BONSAI FOR BEGINNERS

3 SIMPLE STRATEGIES FOR STARTING A BONSAI.
LEARN HOW TO PLANT, GROW, AND CARE FOR YOUR
MINIATURE TREE.

HEAVENLY BONSAI

Copyright © 2023 Heavenly Bonsai. All rights reserved.

The content contained within this book may not be reproduced, duplicated, or transmitted without direct written permission from the author or the publisher.

Under no circumstances will any blame or legal responsibility be held against the publisher, or author, for any damages, reparation, or monetary loss due to the information contained within this book, either directly or indirectly.

Legal Notice:

This book is copyright protected. It is only for personal use. You cannot amend, distribute, sell, use, quote, or paraphrase any part, or the content within this book, without the consent of the author or publisher.

Disclaimer Notice:

Please note the information contained within this document is for educational and entertainment purposes only. All effort has been executed to present accurate, up-to-date, reliable, and complete information. No warranties of any kind are declared or implied. Readers acknowledge that the author is not engaged in the rendering of legal, financial, medical, or professional advice. The content within this book has been derived from various sources. Please consult a licensed professional before attempting any techniques outlined in this book.

By reading this document, the reader agrees that under no circumstances is the author responsible for any losses, direct or indirect, that are incurred as a result of the use of the information contained within this document, including, but not limited to, errors, omissions, or inaccuracies.

CONTENTS

ABOUT THE AUTHOR

For the past several years, Heavenly Bonsai has been a bonsai enthusiast. She stumbled into the world of bonsai and, through trial and error, has learned the craft, maintenance, and styling of bonsai, including watering, fertilizing, repotting, pruning, wiring, and designing. Even after her beginner mistakes, she and her bonsai both made it out alive.

She enjoys reading about bonsai in order to learn new growth and maintenance techniques, as well as the rationale behind them. And through years of meticulous maintenance and love for these lovely, miniature trees, she has mastered the art of caring for bonsai, which she wishes to impart to those who are just starting to appreciate their captivating allure.

She hopes that, by writing this book, she will be able to assist other people who are having trouble caring for their bonsai or are new to the hobby. Everyone can learn how to cultivate and grow lovely bonsai for their charming homes. She wishes for readers to learn from her mistakes while they enjoy creating and growing bonsai of their own.

JOIN OUR BONSAI BEGINNERS COMMUNITY!

We're excited to connect with fellow bonsai lovers and share our passion for cultivating these exquisite miniature trees. By scanning the QR code or clicking the link below, you'll gain access to our private Facebook group. Here, you'll find valuable tips, discussion, and a supportive community of beginners and experts alike.

As a special bonus, members of our group will be the first to receive updates about the author's upcoming books, ensuring you stay ahead in your bonsai journey.

https://bit.ly/HeavenlyBonsai

INTRODUCTION

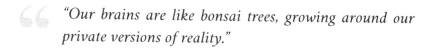 *"Our brains are like bonsai trees, growing around our private versions of reality."*

— SLOANE CROSLEY

We have all heard or read tales about the virtues of perseverance, fortitude, and patience. Stories that inspire us, keep us from giving up, and stress the need to try again and again until we achieve success.

However, all it takes is one little setback to make us give up. One exam failure for us to lose hope for the future. One rejection to feel perpetually discouraged. One unsuccessful bonsai planting made us never want to start over...

One of these difficult situations could very well be the frustration of taking care of a bonsai that was perhaps gifted to you by a loved one, the feeling of failure that comes with not knowing where to start, or the agony of potentially taking away a life.

Is it something you are doing wrong?

Why is it that other people seem to be doing well with their beautiful bonsai while you are the only one struggling?

Or are you scared to even take the first step?

Whatever the case, you can't deny that growing and caring for a bonsai *is* hard. But think of it this way: Cultivating a bonsai tree is not all that different from growing a typical tree. You may be familiar enough to care for a bonsai if you have ever raised a plant by yourself. All you need is water, sunlight, soil, and other additives that any other plant would require to grow. Bonsai is no different in this regard. What is hard, however, is to keep your determination and motivation intact—and this is where you may be having some trouble.

Today, almost everyone can identify a bonsai tree when they see one, but only a few are familiar with the customs and principles that continue to guide how these recognizable miniature plants are supposed to be planted, cultivated, potted, and displayed. That is the art of bonsai. The art that you will be learning and putting to use as you turn each page of this book.

Simply put, bonsai is the technique of growing and shaping the appearance of small, potted trees to resemble older, larger ones. Almost any kind of plant can be turned into a bonsai as long as it is given the right care; however, flexible species like junipers and pines are easier to work with. You can use saplings or seeds to grow your very own bonsai as long as you keep a close eye on their development.

Growing and taking care of a bonsai may be challenging but, in the end, things are only difficult if you think they are!

Even though the art of bonsai has been researched for generations and requires years to perfect, don't let it scare you away from the craft. You don't need some kind of supernatural power or knowledge to successfully grow your own bonsai trees, just a little direction—and you're definitely at the right place for that.

1

KON'NICHIWA BONSAI

K unio Kobayashi, one of the world's best-known bonsai artists, is the owner of a remarkable bonsai tree that stands out for its exceptional age. The unnamed but well-known bonsai tree is thought to be more than 800 years old, and is also one of the most expensive bonsai trees.[1] Kobayashi has received many prestigious awards in Japan, and his 800-year-old bonsai is now displayed at his own nursery, the Shunkaen Bonsai Museum, which is located in Tokyo and is open to visitors.[2]

There are many similar stories and artists that sing the praises of the beautiful and intricate art of growing bonsai. After all, this ancient practice couldn't have lived to this day without a good reason.

WHAT IS BONSAI?

Take a moment and picture a tree. Are you seeing a bunch of trees growing in a field or a park? Or perhaps a big, thick tree that is growing all by itself without any trees nearby? Try to imagine some different types of trees that you may have observed outside. Think about the trees growing in mountainous regions, rocky areas, places where the conditions are challenging for their growth. Imagine a hillside covered with trees, or a tree that is growing next to a river. What about the very old trees whose branches have died as a result of storms, lightning, or perhaps just the passage of time? Or an ancient pine tree with only a small canopy remaining at the top after some of the low branches have died.

All of these pictures of trees, whether in real life or in your mind, serve as the basis for bonsai. A bonsai tree tells a story. It uses the appearance of these natural growing trees to create a small replica or identical miniature tree. It is a form of creative design. Bonsai gives the small tree a story. You employ your creative abilities to guide the miniature tree's growth in the direction that you desire.

The Japanese term "Bon-sai" means "planted in a container" when translated literally. This art style was inspired by a traditional Chinese horticultural technique that was later modified by Japanese Zen Buddhism. This is why the original term for this ancient art was the Chinese word "pun-sai" or "penjing". *Pen* is the Chinese word for pot, while *jing* means scenery or a landscape.

The art of bonsai has existed for over a millennium. Growing a bonsai is ultimately intended to provide a miniature yet accurate reflection of nature in the shape of a tree. And the best part is that bonsai trees can be grown from any kind of tree!

WHY ARE BONSAI GROWN?

People like to grow bonsai for many reasons. One of them is the profound depiction of patience that these miniature trees show us. Given the speed and lack of originality of the modern world, the art of bonsai teaches us to slow down and interact with nature. Having any kind of plants in your home or growing them in your garden, in fact, can help this process and push us to become more introspective. While you cannot hasten the growth of a plant, when it comes to bonsai, we can carefully examine its tenacity and strength as we tenderly tend to it.

For individuals looking for a spiritual experience, bonsai can help infuse a place with spiritual energy. Many traditional forms of mindfulness and meditation have a lot in common with the art of bonsai. Bonsai are cultivated to take on shapes that mirror the harmony and balance in nature, while feng shui, for example, promotes the concept of harmony by achieving a balance between the yin and yang forces present in a space.

Lastly, if you are someone who loves gardening or is fascinated by horticulture, growing bonsai can prove to be a great hobby. It can be grown inside, outdoors, or a combination of both, and it only needs a small amount of soil, water, and space.

At the end of the day, growing a bonsai is nothing less than an emotional commitment. You get to have a lifelong friend, go on a journey together, and be able to care for your little plant just like you would for a pet!

HISTORY OF BONSAI

Even though the practice of bonsai has long been linked to Japan, it actually began in China, before moving to Korea and then Japan.

Around five thousand years ago, people residing in what is now China were creating shallow basins or flattened bowls out of pottery. And a thousand years later, these forms were then rebuilt in bronze for ceremonial use in religion and politics during the Chinese Bronze Age. The Chinese Five Agents Theory, which focuses on the five elements of water, wood, fire, metal, and earth, originated the notion of the power of miniature copies 2,300 years ago. For instance, a learner could concentrate on a mountain's magical qualities and obtain access to them by making a scaled-down version of it. The more magical power a reproduction had, the smaller it was likely to be compared to the original.

Under the Han Emperor, due to freshly opened trade with its neighbors, new aromatics and incense were imported. Incense burners in the shape of mountain peaks that soared above the waters were developed as a new sort of vessel to represent the mythical Islands of the Blessed, which were then thought to be the homes of the immortals. Some of these burners, which were typically made of metal, ceramic, or bronze, rested on little dishes, either to catch burning embers or to hold a tiny symbolic ocean. These burners' detachable lids frequently featured stylized depictions of mythical characters scaling forested hills. The incense smoke rose from the cave entrances via the lid perforations, much like the ethereal vapors in the actual mountains. It's possible that some later stone lids may have been discovered already covered with lichens or moss, creating realistic miniature landscapes.

The first tray sceneries are thought to have been transported from China to Japan as religious mementos at least 1,200 years ago.

In China and Japan, bonsai has changed and grown in distinct ways. Chinese bonsai is still firmly rooted in the past. The Japanese styles, on the other hand, are more esthetically beautiful and organic. The Japanese bonsai are generally more elegant and well-kept, and each variety has its own distinctive charms and admirers.

Lastly, we owe a huge debt of gratitude to the Chinese and Japanese artists for creating this exquisite work and preserving it for close to 2,500 years. We wouldn't be able to enjoy bonsai as we do now without their passion, creative tradition, and diligent maintenance.

IDENTIFYING YOUR BONSAI

It is crucial to understand how to recognize a bonsai tree so you can give it the right attention and upkeep that it requires. Certain tree species may have particular needs for sunshine, soil, nutrients, irrigation, pruning, shaping, and training. While some bonsai trees are simple to maintain, others may require specialized care. And you won't know the fundamentals of caring for a bonsai tree if you don't know what kind of tree you are taking care of!

When learning how to recognize a bonsai tree, there are a number of things to consider. You can begin by figuring out whether the tree is a deciduous or an evergreen one.

To identify an evergreen tree, you can look at its leaves. Even during the dry and cold season, evergreen trees retain their green leaves. These trees have smaller leaves that shed gradually over the spring and summer as opposed to shedding all at once. Evergreen trees are found in tropical regions like the rainforest, and there are only a handful of evergreen trees, usually conifers, that can survive the bitter cold in regions with hard winters. The leaves usually have a wax-like coating. Even though evergreen trees don't have flowers, they can nevertheless generate cones that contain their seed.

For deciduous trees, warm and extended growing seasons with lots of humidity are necessary. These trees require nutrient-rich soil, a significant amount of filtered light, and at most five hours of sunlight directly every day. During the fall season, these trees tend to shed their leaves, and when the weather gets colder, they enter their inactive or dormant phase. Deciduous trees are renowned for their vibrant foliage and fresh appearance, which is especially apparent in the autumn when their leaves are just about to fall off. The palette of the leaves includes red, orange, purple, and yellow, among other colors.

TYPES OF BONSAI

Ficus

Ficus Bonsai

Despite the fact that most people connect bonsai with indoor decorations, several types actually thrive outside—though this can make taking up the bonsai art difficult for people who live in colder climates. Fortunately, some trees (like the ficus, for example) can survive inside. The two types with visually appealing trunks that are most suitable for indoor gardening are Ficus retusa and Ficus ginseng. The capacity of ficus trees to adapt well to growing constraints is what makes them so flexible. The key to limiting plant size in bonsai is to choose a tiny container. Ficus trees make excellent bonsai because they thrive in smaller containers. They can also overlook neglect in terms of watering and other aspects of upkeep. For example, ficus plants can often tolerate the dry conditions found in indoor settings. Just be sure to place your small ficus in a bright area where the sun shines.

Juniper

Juniper Bonsai

In a miniature form, this needle-leaved tree looks really lovely and attractive. However, it is crucial to remember that junipers struggle indoors. So, instead of using them as indoor decorations, consider cultivating these bonsai trees outside. You would have to put them in a location where they will receive at least four hours of sunlight each day. The juniper tree can withstand freezing temperatures, unlike other, less durable bonsai-friendly trees.

Junipers are also resistant to pests, much like the other types of bonsai trees that are deemed suitable for beginners. But keep in mind that juniper bonsai can still be targeted by webworms and spider mites. Luckily, pruning on a regular basis can help prevent pests and keep leaves from piling up. And here's a fun fact: juniper bonsai are usually thought to be ideal for beginners because of their tolerance for over-pruning! This means that these bonsai will eventually recover from improper pruning, even though it may initially weaken them and produce browning.

Rosemary

You can choose a rosemary plant to grow as a bonsai if you also enjoy some tasty, delicious form of art! By that, we mean that when you prune a rosemary bonsai, you can also net some herbs for culinary purposes, and the best part is that it will also aid in maintaining the plant's shape. Rosemary plants require regular watering to grow, but they are also susceptible to having their roots rot, so make sure that you maintain them in a pot with adequate drainage.

Rosemary Bonsai

Remember to remove any new growth that occurs after the first set of leaves in order to keep the plant at its small size. A rosemary plant won't overrun its pot if the roots are cut by at least 25 percent. You can use wiring to shape the branches of this bonsai as long as they are young and elastic enough. The ability to swiftly grow rosemary from seed is another benefit of using it as your miniature tree!

Chinese Elm

Chinese Elm Bonsai

If you are a beginner to bonsai art, you should start with this slow-growing plant because it can thrive in practically any place. Chinese elms can survive outside, which means they can be cultivated and taken care of both inside and out. You only have to pick a location that receives plenty of early sunlight and also gradually gives way to shade in the late afternoon. Another factor that makes Chinese elm trees ideal for bonsai is how simple they are to shape and prune, mostly due to the relatively slower speed of their growth. Again, apart from the infestation of spider mites, these trees are also not very prone to pests.

2

THE SOIL AND NUTRITION

Now plants are living beings, but they depend on humans to take care of them. Just like a human needs air and nutrition to live a healthy life, a plant needs air, water, soil, and nourishment to grow. While bonsai cultivation is a beautiful art, it does require tremendous effort, as you must know by now. The expenses, if set aside, pave the way to new intricacies as you move in the direction of growing a bonsai.

One central element one must focus on when walking the route to cultivating a bonsai is the soil. A bonsai's roots are like the engine of a car. If you don't get this right, the functioning of the rest of the car is havoc in disguise. In this light, the caretaker of a bonsai can be comparable to a teenager. Like a teenager is concerned mainly about how the car looks rather than its mechanics, some folks focus on the appearance of their bonsai rather than its vitality.

So, suppose you plan on nurturing your bonsai in the best ways possible. In that case, you must direct the focus toward the soil. Selecting the wrong soil for your bonsai can have dire consequences.

Conversely, if one uses the correct soil and impeccable horticultural practices, the tree can be completely reformed. More so, our passion for the cultivation process will also be beyond bounds.

In this chapter section, we will walk through the basics of soil, water and drainage. These will provide the base for you as we further explore soil and nutrition options in this chapter.

Nourishment and soil are the building pillars of a tree. If done right, the tree can live up to 800 years of age.

SOIL MIXTURE

A bonsai tree, in order to grow, requires a soil mixture. This step is one of the most crucial ones when it comes to cultivating perfection. Soil is imperative to trees for nutrition, but your tree also requires proper drainage, aeration and the ability to retain water. See, plants lose a lot of water in the form of transpiration.

The process is a two-edged sword, and to grow a bonsai, the soil must be filled with nutrition that matches up with the water demand of the plant. One can find ready-mixed soils from the shops around them, but preparing soil mixture at home gives control over the material and saves money as well.

If you make the soil mixture at home, you will know the exact mixture that is required for your particular tree species.

BONSAI SUBSTRATES

The quality of soil used for a bonsai directly affects the health and strength of the tree. In ages past, it has been found that unhealthy trees that lack strength are the ones that have been planted in poor bonsai soil.[1]

In some cases, they have been planted in average garden soil. See, bonsai cultivation is an art, and it requires dedication. The type of soil that one uses for caretaking their bonsai can lead either to healthy growth or impediments. If a person decides to use garden soil for their bonsai, it will limit the bonsai's growth.

There are certain factors that make the soil suitable for the bonsai. Let us walk through these.

WATER RETENTION

In order for soil to be good for the bonsai, it needs to be able to soak in the water and retain sufficient amounts. This is imperative for the nutrition of the plant between watering. However, too much water retention will result in damage. Therefore, drainage is essential too.[2]

DRAINAGE

The rule of nature applies to plants like all other living beings. Too much of anything, whether it is oxygen, nitrogen, water or carbon, can lead to deterioration. For a bonsai to grow appropriately, excess water must be drained immediately from the pot. If excessive water is retained, it will lead to rotting of the roots and kill the tree. Soils which do not drain adequately lack aeration and are susceptible to a buildup of salts.

AERATION

The particles that are reused in a bonsai mix need to be big enough to allow tiny gaps, or air pockets, to exist between each particle of the soil.[3] These provide oxygen for the roots, good bacteria and mycorrhizae. In essence, this allows for the food to be processed before it is absorbed by the tree's root hairs and sent to the leaves for the purpose of photosynthesis.

ORGANIC OR INORGANIC SOILS

There exist two types of soil mixes in the world; organic or inorganic. Organic soil components include dead plant matter like peat, leaf litter or bark. The potential problem associated with organic soil components is that organic matter breaks down and decreases plant drainage over time.

Different organic components tend to deteriorate at varying speeds, so it is hard to say how quickly an organic soil mix will become harmful to the plant. If the cultivator of a bonsai tree is adamant about using organic soil mixtures, it's suggested to use one that utilizes pine bark.

The majority of the time, potting composts tend to absorb water extremely poorly when they are completely dry. This is one of the major problems encountered with cheap indoor bonsai trees that are purchased at garden centres. One may think that they watered the plant appropriately, but the water may run past the soil to the bottom of the pot.

This is a menace in itself, and in order to avoid it, one needs to be careful about the pot type they are choosing, the soil that is being utilized, and the place that the bonsai is being brought by. All of these contribute to the overarching process of bonsai cultivation.

In contrast to organic soil components, inorganic soil components tend to contain little to no organic matter. These include volcanic lava, calcite, and baked/fired clay. These tend to absorb few nutrients and little water as compared to their organic counterparts. Still, these are absolutely great in terms of drainage and aeration. The limited absorption capacity of the inorganic soil gives the cultivator control over the amount of fertilizer that will be sown in the soil.

An inorganic, particle-based, well-structured soil leads to quick water drainage. It allows fresh air to continually enter the soil. On the contrary, a compacted form of organic soil that lacks structure leads to a lack of aeration and drainage. As a result, the fate is the overall deterioration of the tree's health. Without swift action, the roots will eventually rot, thereby killing the bonsai tree.

WATER—BASICS FOR BONSAI

A plant needs water for a variety of purposes; these include transportation and utilization of nutrients. The majority of the time, water is absorbed through the roots. However, too much of anything is harmful in nature.

Some exceptions exist in plants wherein they can survive despite being completely submerged in water; more often than not, most plants cannot. The reason that trees cannot survive excessive water in the soil is due to the lack of oxygen.

Simply put, the majority of plants tend to absorb humidity from the soil, not water. Therefore, damp but not wet soil is required for optimum health and growth. After watering bonsai, the core requirement is to drain the excess water from the pot, leaving the soil moist but not soaking in nature.

DRAINAGE OF SOIL

In the search to find the perfect growing medium for a bonsai, it is imperative that drainage be maintained. Drainage, in simple terms, is the process in which excess water escapes the growing medium. There exist multiple factors that affect the drainage of water from the soil.

After watering the plant, it is essential that the liquid water is removed from the soil quickly. This is in relation to the health of the plant, which needs oxygen to survive. The entire process in this regard is dependent upon gravity. Water, as nature would have it, has surface tension, because of which it clings to surfaces.

Despite the pull of gravity, some of it flows down, but the rest of it stays on the surface it has been thrown on. In similar essence, soil comprises a lot of particles with small spaces between them. If put simply, the more closely packed the particles are, the less drainage will be achieved because the water has a lot of surfaces upon which to hold. Therefore, gravity is unable to pull the water down to the core.

Conversely, if the pores of spaces are larger, the water will pass through the soil and drain out. In order for a bonsai tree to survive and thrive, it is essential that a balance of drainage is achieved. It is indeed one of the key factors through which the perfect soil or growing media for a bonsai can be achieved.

Unfortunately, one of the most difficult questions to answer is in relation to how much drainage is appropriate for a plant since there are many variables, including the fact that every plant has different water needs and respiration rates. Drainage also has an impact on how fast a plant grows. Young plants often tend to grow faster than an old and mature bonsai tree.

If an old bonsai tree is provided with extensively free drainage soil, then that would inadvertently lead to excessive nutrition, which would, as a result, exceed the vigor required by the bonsai. As a result, what would incur is coarse growth, long internodes and excessively large foliage. This, as a result, would abruptly spoil the esthetic of the bonsai and upset its balance.

Understanding the principles involved in the intricacy of bonsai growth allows for an overall good starting point. Over the years, the plant growing medium can be adjusted in order to provide the perfect solution.

Porosity of Soil

Similar to how humans live inside their houses, the roots of a plant live between the solid soil particles. The term that is used for the amount of air held in a growing medium is Air Filled Porosity (AFP). Solid particles also comprise a certain amount of air if they are porous in nature.

Soil is composed of particles with varying-sized spaces. In general, the small spaces—called micropores—between the solid particles of soil contain water. However, it is minute to the extent that the finest of root hairs cannot access it.

Another form of space is middle-sized pores or mesopores. They contain water that is available to plants and air that moves into these as the plant removes excess water. Pores that are greater than 0.1 mm in diameter are called macropores and they allow free air circulation within a short span of watering.

Ideally, the number of mesopores should be higher to ensure good water retention. Moreover, micropores should also be present in sufficient quantities to allow free drainage, gaseous exchange and a thorough form of root exploration. The perfect form of growing medium/soil will maintain a high proportion of air-filled pores without restricting the water supply.

Other Drainage Factors

While the factors that have been discussed so far have an extensive impact on bonsai and its growth, other drainage factors also have a role. One such factor is called the "capillary action."[4] Capillary action or capillarity refers to the phenomenon in which liquid spontaneously rises in a narrow space like a thin tube or in porous materials.

The thinner the size of the capillary (tube), the higher water will rise. If the conditions are ideal, capillary action allows water to overcome gravity, and water moves uphill. As a result, the drainage of the soil will cease altogether.

The role of the soil used is different in summer than in winter. The medium chosen for growing a bonsai is influenced by many factors. These include the shape/depth of the container, the individual customized needs of the tree species, the age of the bonsai, the type of growth that is required, and the environmental conditions.

Other factors like watering times, use of fertilizer, and pH also have an impact when it comes to maintaining the role of the soil in summer and winter alike.

ORGANIC VERSUS INORGANIC BONSAI SOIL

There exist two forms of soils, these are organic and inorganic in nature.

Inorganic Soil

Just like the name suggests, this form of soil has no organic component in it. This implies that any nutrient that the tree requires will be added via fertilization because the soil does not contain any inherent nutrients.

Three types of inorganic substrates are usually mixed together to make bonsai soil. These are:

- Pumice
- Lava rock
- Akadama

Pumice

This volcanic rock is lightweight and porous in nature. It tends to retain some amount of water but typically forms the dry part of a bonsai soil mix.[5]

Lava Rock

Another volcanic rock, this one provides quality water retention for the bonsai soil mix using its porous properties.[6]

Akadama

This clay is made in Japan and is the primary component in soil mixes. It is used to hold water in the mix.

Organic Soil

Some bonsai soil mixes include organic compounds that leak peat or bark. These elements are used to add nutrients to the soil. They can also break down and inhibit drainage. Due to this reason, the popularity of this organic soil is slowly decreasing.

SOIL COMPONENTS

Some commonly used soil components that one may find are detailed in this section of the chapter.[7]

Kanuma

This material is remarkably light, pale, soft, and yellow. It is volcanic in nature. It is found in Japan and serves as an acidic material that is best suitable for growing ericas. The typical pH for this one is 5.5.[8] It has a soft, airy structure that allows roots to penetrate through the particles.

Kiryu

Kiryu is a hard, heavy Japanese type of dense pumice which is moderately absorbent in nature. It has a neutral pH. It has a hard frost-proof structure which means it is long-lived and suitable for bonsai-like pines that are rarely repotted.[9]

Ezo Grit

This one is Japanese volcanic pumice with an attractive buff color. It has a good moisture holding capacity and is also frost proof, so it tends to live long. It has low C.E.C (cation exchange capacity). Moreover, Ezo Grit is moderately heavy and expensive due to transportation costs.

Fuji Grit/Sand

This is a jet-black crushed volcanic lava ash.[10] It has a very attractive color and is moderately absorbent but very heavy.

Horticultural Grit

Horticultural grit is available in various forms like fine sand and gravel. In essence, it is basically a crushed stone that is normally quartzite or granite. It is generally used for the purpose of digging in heavy clay soils and opening up the soils in raised beds.

John Innes Mixes

These are carefully formulated loam or peat-based compost mixes that are specifically designed for general horticultural use. These work well in conventional flowerpot-style containers.

Perlite

Perlite is a soil material manufactured through volcanic glass, heated at a high temperature of 850-900°C. It tends to expand rapidly, up to seven to sixteen times its original volume and forms an ultra-lightweight, hard, but highly absorbent material. It is extremely popular in horticulture and is used to improve drainage. Perlite also reduces the weight of conventional composts, wherein it is mixed at a volume of 10 percent.

Peat

The primary feature of peat is its ability to hold water. However, using it can be tumultuous.

Cat Litter

Cat litter is available in various forms, and its use within the bonsai cultivation has increased notches. Cat litter based on fired clay material tends to provide a perfect growing media when mixed with other materials. Cat litter is cheap and readily available. However, it has one overriding concern, which is related to the use of deodorizers and disinfectants. Some prominent brands consider cat litter to be perfectly okay to grow plants, but it is important to bear in mind that cat litter is not designed for this use.

If the manufacturer or supermarket brand owner modifies the material or composition of the material within the bag, whether it happens due to increasing costs or health concerns, the risk to the health of a bonsai tree significantly increases.

Another important factor that is worth consideration is the pH. This is of absolutely no concern to cat littering, but it can have a profound impact on the bonsai. Most cat litters either tend to be extremely acidic or alkaline.

Thereby it is thoroughly recommended to always use horticulture-certified materials that are guaranteed to fulfil their function. You see, the loss of one tree will offset the savings you have made by using cat litter.

Bark Products

There are a lot of bark-based products available for horticultural use that tend to range from sublime to absolute trash. Sorting through the good and bad requires extensive effort and knowledge. The bark is obtained from forestry, logging, and sawmill operations. Various species of tree bark tend to provide different growing environments for plants.

Composted Bark

Good quality composted bark is a finely fibrous and spongy material that holds a lot of moisture. It is extremely helpful as a part of the soil mix added for the purpose of moisture retention.[11]

However, in winter, it can end up holding a lot of water and, as a result, may lead to oxygen starvation which will eventually cause root rot. Therefore using it sparingly is recommended.

Depending on the source, composted bark can be a top-notch product for adding to blended bonsai soil. Some cheaper forms of composted bark, however, are little more than shredded composted garden waste from domestic waste streams with a little bark added.

Other bark products may have large volumes of wood and cambium, which can make the product very wet and slimy. In fact, products can vary to the extent that composed bark can prove to be a minefield.

Top-quality composted bark is just a form of carefully graded bark from forestry operators and sawmills, which is cleaned, composted slowly over a long period of time, and accurately graded.

Chipped Bark

Bonsai soil mix requires top-quality graded pine bark, which has less than 3 percent wood fiber. Chipper bark ideally should have little fines (dust) and offer a high AFP (air-filled porosity). The pH for the material will be around 5, and when mixed with other products, it would help to buffer the pH, especially if it is mixed with hard water.

Inherently it has a poor nutrient-holding capacity and less nutrition, but it has the capability of holding water. It can provide a warm and airy rhizosphere with a nice springy soil mix which can help bring bonsai through a hard freezing winter.

Top-quality bark provides the perfect medium to propagate the cuttings. Bark also seems extremely good at encouraging mycorrhiza to flush. The highest quality of chipped bark products is composed of orchid cultivation; however, these are typically highly coarse to use in bonsai pots.

Lapillo

Lapillo is an element that forms during volcanic eruptions and is a term used to describe small particles that explode in the environment. After the explosion, they cool on their descent back to earth. It is ideal to use lapilli with other bonsai soil products for the best results.[12]

Supalite Fine

A lightweight fired clay aggregate that serves as a great ingredient when mixed with other bonsai soil types. Its honeycomb structure allows for the retention of a great amount of water, along with promoting exceptional air circulation.

Supalite Black

An ultra-lightweight fired clay product that holds the same open honeycomb structure. When it is mixed with other soil media, it promotes drainage, increases air capacity, and dramatically reduces the overall weight. It is frost-proof in nature and tends to resist breaking down for multiple years.

Horticultural Moler

A fired clay product that is produced from naturally occurring montmorillonite, it is formed from ancient algae deposits. Horticultural moler tends to create a lightweight, porous, and granular material.

Horticultural Zeolite

Natural zeolites are bound to form when volcanic rocks and layers react with alkaline groundwater. These have a porous structure and have the capability of holding up to 60 percent of their volume in water.

Graded Horticultural Charcoal

Green Dream Bonsai Biochar is a favourable component of growth media for bonsai plants. It improves moisture retention while also allowing for good drainage capabilities. It has the capability of retaining significant nutrients from fertilizers.

MIXING RATIOS

Different tree species demand a different form soil-mixture ratio. However, there exist two main mixtures that are re-used for deciduous or coniferous trees. Both comprise akadama for water retention quality, pumice for good substrate structure, and lava rock for aeration and drainage.

Remember that both mixtures can and should always be customised as per your need, circumstances and location. If your schedule is busy and you know you won't be able to make time for your trees twice a day, then try to add more akadama.

The following ratios are a general guide only. In wet climatic areas, individuals should add more lava rock or grit to the bonsai soil. This tends to enhance the drainage quality of the mixture.

The mixing ratio of the substrates tends to vary. For conifers like pine and juniper, the mixture is typically a 1:1:1 ratio which means 1 part akadama, 1 part lava rock, and 1 part pumice.[13] For deciduous trees like elms and maples, the mixture tends to be slightly different. The ratio is 2:1:1, which means 2 parts akadama, 1 part lava rock, and 1 part pumice.

Mixture for Conifers 1:1:1 Ratio

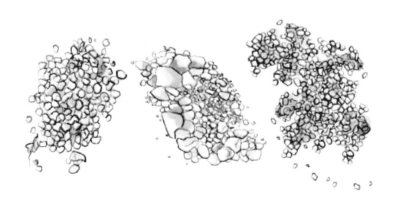

From left to right: 1 part Akadama, 1 part
Lava Rock, and 1 part Pumice

For deciduous bonsai soil, it is suggested to use 50 percent akadama, 25 percent pumice, and 25 percent lava rock. For coniferous and pine soil, it is suggested to use 33 percent akadama, 33 percent pumice, and 33 percent lava rock.[14]

HOW TO MIX BONSAI SUBSTRATE

Now that you have an understanding of the components that can be used and the ratio for each, it is time you gain knowledge about mixing the bonsai substrate.

Right Equipment

Apart from the components that build up a bonsai tree's soil, it is imperative that you have the right equipment.[15] This will allow you to gain the best outcomes from the materials you have picked.

The material you ordered will come in bags or sacks with major impurities like dust. Other impurities include grass, and the possibility other forms of organic matter will be present as well. These cause damage to the overall product and thereby require removal.

To make it easy for the user, a swifter can be used to sift through the material at various levels. This will allow you to have smaller granules for smaller potted bonsai and larger granules for larger bonsai. Sifting is not necessarily an important step, but it is highly recommended.

The Mixing Recipe

There exists no one way in which you should approach your own unique mix. There are a lot of guidelines for the approach, but these are all mere suggestions.

As a bonsai hobbyist, it is important that you experience the mix before dismissing or criticizing it. Remember, what works for you may or may not work for someone else. Since there exists a clear guideline for the type of bonsai and its mixture, the one that you formulate should correlate with the type of tree.

Clump and Loose

Naturally, the soil you have made will condense after some time, and this condensing action will be stimulated to test how well the soil holds up. In order to facilitate that type of compaction, even before filling the pot with a bonsai mix, one should squeeze a big clump of wetted mix in their hand.

If the mix compacts in the form of a dense, hard clump, it is possibly filled with organic matter and can retain a lot of moisture. This can, as a result, lead to a lot of problems. Moreover, air will be unable to penetrate through this type of soil.

On the contrary, if the mix falls away once you release it from your palm, it is a good, well-draining mix. In order to correct too loose or too compact a form of soil, you will need to simply add to the mix either more grit or more organic matter that fits your needs.

QUANTITY OF SOIL

As someone who is designing their own oil mixture for the bonsai tree, it is important to know the quantity of soil you would be using. The simple answer in relation to the amount of soil that should be present in pots is that it should be enough to support the plants growing in them and to elevate the plants to an adequate height.

For height, it is meant that the bonsai plant should reach a position from which all light and air can reach it easily. Moreover, the soil should be present far enough below the rim of the planter so that it won't spill out when plants are watered.

When deciding about the quantity of soil that needs to be purchased, it is best to consider the factor of soil compression that commonly results due to moistening and pressing the soil in the pot. **Due to soil compression, you will need to add 15-20 percent more dry soil to the container.**

Also, remember that if you transfer a plant from one pot to another, you will be transferring some soil present around its root as well.

NUTRIENTS REQUIRED FOR SOIL

In order to achieve a successful growth factor in the bonsai, it is important that "base soiling" is incurred. The term describes the process of adding nutrients to the soil prior to planting. Extrapolation of this concept in the world is exceptionally common. Many think that bonsai soil needs to be "rich" in some way. The nutrients that are required by a bonsai tree should be supplied in a controlled manner using fertilizers, ideally organic products.

Humus

Bonsai soil does not require inherent nutrient content. All the nutrient requirements of a bonsai are taken care of by regular use of fertilizers. One of the most important elements in bonsai soil is humus. However, composted organic material is not humus. Humus is actually what is left after an organic material has completely decayed. It is a black substance that typically turns topsoil black. Humus has a high cation exchange capacity.[16] So when you mix compost in the soil, the nutrient holding capacity of the soil will increase in time. The organic material, however, is a means to an end but not the end in itself.

CATION EXCHANGE CAPACITY (CEC)

Bonsai that grow in small volumes of soil are heavily reliant on the growing medium to retain the nutrients. A soil's ability to hold on to nutrients is known as the cation exchange capacity. The nutrients of a plant are present in the form of chemical compounds that can be easily washed away due to a poorly structured soil mix.

Remember, bonsai that grow in soil with a good CEC tend to look healthy, with strong, uniform leaf growth. Over the growing periods, they grow to be strong across their branches without weak points.

SOIL FLORA AND FAUNA

Soil not only supports the plants but also provides a home for countless tiny life forms that include a bewildering array of fungi, bacteria, and insect life. A single gram of garden soil tends to contain a million fungi, such as yeast and molds. While some of these can be detrimental to the tree, a vast number are crucial to its well-being.

A balanced soil is one where plants grow in an active and vibrant environment. The mineral content within the soil and the physical structure are important for the well-being of the tree, but it is essentially the life in the earth that tends to power the cycle and provide fertility.

If soil organisms are absent, organic material will accumulate and litter the soil surface. As a result, there would be no food for the plants. Among this fauna, one of the key roles is played by fungi and bacteria. These act as decomposers that break down organic material like fertilizer to produce detritus and other breakdown products.

Soil detritivores like earthworms tend to ingest detritus and decompose it. Saprotrophs are represented by fungi and bacteria that extract soluble nutrients, which in turn can be absorbed by plants.

SOIL PH

The pH of soil influences the growth of a plant extensively. The pH scale is basically a means of expressing the degree of acidity or alkalinity. The scale is from 0 to 14, with 7 being neutral, 0 being extremely acidic, and 14 being extremely alkaline. This means that soil with a pH of 6 is more acidic than pH 7.[17]

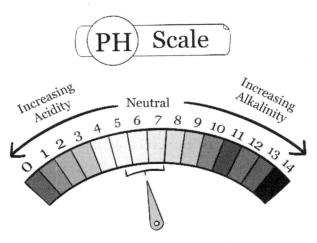

Ideal for most bonsai species

A pH of 6-6.5 is ideal for most bonsai, which is slightly acidic in nature. Alkaline conditions of the soil are created by the presence of calcium (lime) in the soil. The pH of soil heavily influences the availability of nutrients. For example, a very acidic soil will restrict the availability of nitrogen. Therefore getting the pH right is the core to getting the plant to thrive.

The pH levels of plants are influenced by water and the type of fertilizer that is used. Adjusting pH levels is a tricky thing to do, and in the case of bonsai, it is not recommended. The best plan of action that is recommended is to determine the pH of the plant and select a soil medium that is correct at the outset.

If you have ever encountered plants that show a continued reduction in growth performance over several seasons with impaired flowering and foliage, then chances are that the pH of the soil is not appropriate.

If you are in doubt about the particular needs of a plant, then it is a good idea to start with a professionally produced bonsai soil mix with a pH of around 6.5. Ericas like azaleas and heathers need a mix around pH 5.5.

HOW DOES PH CHANGE?

The pH of the bonsai soil changes with water, fertilizer and soil type. When talking about the pH of the soil, it is important to consider the influence of these factors in detail.[18]

Influence of Water

Generally, bonsai prefer slightly acidic water with a pH below 7.0. Municipal water is commonly basic (pH above 7.0). The higher the pH, the harder it is to keep the bonsai healthy. There exists no perfect pH for irrigation water as the optimal pH for a given nutrient is different from another.

Some high pH water that can be used for bonsai include rainwater, vinegar and siphon mixer. If you are looking forward to acidifying your water for the bonsai, then use a siphon system like Hozon Brass Siphon Mixer, which has the ability to draw acidic solution from a reservoir and automatically mix it with the water coming from the spigot.

Influence of Fertilizer

The pH of soil may change because of the fertilizer used. Fertilizers are an essential component for trees because they provide strong nutrients for growth and help in balancing the pH levels of bonsai soils.

The pH level of the majority of bonsai needs to be around 6-6.5 when it comes to growth. If the bonsai gets extremely alkaline in nature, it can lead to burned leaves. This is usually due to the quality of water or lack of fertilizer. Bonsai fertilizers have sulphate, and these are ideal for bringing the soil pH level back to the ideal.

WAYS TO TEST SOIL PH

If you are wondering how you could test the pH of the soil, then some methods come in handy. These are as follows:

Testing with a commercial test probe

To use a commercial test probe to test the soil pH, you will need to dig a hole in the soil. You can dig the hole using a trowel or spade. The hole should be 2-4 inches (5.1-10.2 cm) deep. In the hole, break down the soil and remove twigs and foreign debris.

Fill the hole to the brim until you have a muddy pool in the bottom. Then fill the hole with water. Use distilled (not spring) water. This can be obtained from your local pharmacy. Remember, rainwater is slightly acidic, and tap water is usually slightly alkaline.

Then insert the test probe into the mud. It is important to ensure that the tester is clean and calibrated (for exact measurements). Then you will need to wipe the probe using a tissue or clean cloth and insert in the mud.

Hold it there for a minimum of sixty seconds and take a reading. pH usually gets measured on a scale of 1-14, although the tester may have a different range.

- A pH of 7 indicates neutral soil.
- A pH above 7 indicates alkaline soil.
- A pH below 7 indicates acidic soil.

pH Test Strip

You can choose to test the pH of the soil using test strips. These are also known as litmus paper and are one of the easiest and quickest ways to measure the pH of the soil. These can be purchased online or at your local garden store.

What you need to do is mix a handful of soil with room-temperature distilled water. Then take a handful of the soil which you would like to test and put it in a bowl. Then put some of the distilled water in the bowl until the dirt has the consistency of a milkshake. You can then stir the mixture to ensure that the water has been fully incorporated.

Try to hold the pH test strip at the non-reading end, and then for twenty to thirty seconds, dip the strip within the dirt mixture. The test time can vary significantly, so be sure to follow the specific directions on the test strip you are using to gauge the adequate dipping time. When the time is over, remove the pH strip from the water. Then dip it for a short time in distilled water and clean off the dirt.

You can then compare the pH strip to the test kit's key. See the key included in the test kit to read the pH. Normally the key is color coded. The color will correspond to the pH.

SOIL FOR BONSAI TREES

There are certain forms of soil that are best suited for bonsai trees. Bonsai trees have the capability of growing well in home-made bonsai soils with basic components such as bark chips and gravel. This DIY bonsai soil can provide enough porosity and water retention to allow the bonsai to grow.

However, there exist special soil requirements for bonsai depending on the type of bonsai one plans to grow. Imported soils from Japan, like akadama, kanuma and Kiryu, tend to provide ideal growing conditions for bonsai.

The clay granular akadama soil is best suited for bonsai trees. For bonsai plants that grow in acidic environments, such as azaleas, kanuma is best suited. Kiryu, on the contrary, is best suited for pines and junipers.

The irony associated with the term "bonsai soil" is the fact that there isn't really any "soil" in most of the bonsai soil mixes. Instead, what exists is actually a mixture of substrates like crushed lava rock, which resembles gravel more than soil. In this type of mix, the bonsai tree is provided with an environment that allows for feeder roots to develop. As a result, the tree can thrive more easily.

Now that you have a fair idea about the quantity of soil that will be required, it is time you decide on the kind of pots that you will use for a bonsai plant. In the next chapter, we will discuss just that.

3

THINKING POTS

As a bonsai hobbyist, one of the most pivotal things to know about is the pot that you select. The pot of your bonsai will determine a lot of aspects of your plant. So, if you are ready to dive deep into the world of bonsai art, then let's take a look at the qualities that you need to consider when selecting a pot for your bonsai.

While the tree itself contributes one-half of the composition, the pot completes the image. The bonsai in its literal sense is judged by its visual impact of both the tree and the pot. Unfortunately, the majority of bonsai hobbyists find it difficult to choose and locate the correct and best pot to plant their bonsai tree in.

The downside of choosing a poor design of pot is that it can lessen the impact of the plant; conversely, a well-chosen pot would strengthen the plant. Ultimately, unless the "perfect" pot is found, a bonsai tree will never reach its full potential.

A pot can sometimes prove to be an expensive investment since finding one that is unsuitable for your needs means that, in the long run, you will have to search for that one perfect pot for your plant. Finding the right pot at the right time is not only satisfying, but it also helps in saving money, along with helping avoid a pile of pots that don't suit your tree.

CHOOSING THE RIGHT POT

As previously said, choosing the right pot is not an easy job. Along with the mundane factory-made Chinese and Korean pots, you can find a diverse range of bonsai potters and potteries throughout the world.

These individuals tend to offer diverse pot designs and glazes for the enthusiasts of bonsai art. With a wide array of choices in terms of color, size, and design, it can become exceptionally difficult to choose the best pot for the tree.

Pot choice is also subjective in nature since, ultimately, the final decision will be made according to a person's personal taste. Some enthusiasts tend to prefer pot shapes and textures with glazes that are conservative. In contrast, others prefer more unusual, personal choices.

This chapter section will be divided into four parts to choose the correct pot for your tree. These are pot dimension, pot shape, pot color, and texture.

POT DIMENSION AND SIZE

Pot Depth should be equal to the width of the trunk at the base of the soil

Pot Length should be equal to 1/2 to 2/3 the height of the tree

The general rule for the depth of the pot is that it should be the same as the diameter of the trunk right above the soil surface.

- If you want to go for oval or rectangular pots, then the length of the pot should be two-thirds of the height of the tree.
- If round pots are what you are looking for, then your preference should be one-third of the height of the tree.
- If the bonsai tree that you are trying to attain is one with wide canopies, then a wider pot would be necessary, and this can be compensated for by using a slightly shallow pot.

- If the tree you are planning to opt for has a very thick trunk, then it might be appropriate to have a slightly deeper but narrow pot.

POT SHAPE

The shape of a pot can be masculine or feminine. A masculine tree is one that radiates an aura of strength. It may have a heavily tapered trunk, be craggy, have a mature bark, strong angular branching, or it may have deadwood. There may also be a straight, powerful trunk or a dense canopy.

A feminine tree, on the other hand, will be one that has a more delicate appearance, and sinuous movement in its trunk and branches. This one will have a light canopy and a slow taper.

Some tree species tend to be predisposed toward being considered feminine or masculine in nature. Pines or angular hawthorns tend to be considered masculine in nature, while Japanese maples are considered feminine.

However, if you have a heavily tapered Japanese maple with delicate leaves and branching, then this could be a feminine species with masculine features. On the other hand, a tall hawthorn with craggy, rough bark, gentle curves, and gradual taper can be considered masculine with feminine characteristics.

If the pot is deep with strong angular features, then it is masculine, whereas if it is shallow with soft lines, then it is feminine in nature.

Strong chunks and deep rectangles with sharp corners on pots represent masculine quality, as do square pots.

In terms of selecting the shape of the pot, you need to be aware of the basics. If you choose to opt for a rectangular pot, then these are best for coniferous species and colossal deciduous trees that have extensively pronounced taper, wide bases, and heavily buttressed nebari (visible roots). These types of pots are appropriate for trees that have a more masculine outlook.

Oval pots are ones that are suitable for reflecting the femininity associated with deciduous trees, clump-style bonsai, groves, and forests. The lesser the taper of a tree is, the more feminine in nature it becomes; sinuous curves also tend to dampen the masculinity of a tree.

Trees that are tall, straight, or sinuously curved with extremely little taper tend to be ones with the most feminine qualities, and pots that suit this kind of tree are ones that are shallow.

POT FEET

The main purpose associated with the feet of a pot for bonsai is to allow good drainage and airflow. However, feet can also be used to change the appearance of a pot. Feet can either be subtle or decorative. These can also be made to look strong and robust

These qualities can be used to exclusively customize the overall feel of the pot. For example, if the pot you choose has big chunky feet, then this will add an element of strength to the overall design, while delicate feet will have the opposite effect.

POT COLOR

Once you have decided upon the structure of the pot, the next thing you will need to focus on is the color and texture. Each individual tree is unique, as no two trees are identical. There are always some variations between trees, and these can be highlighted through pot color and texture.

The color of the pot can be picked up along with a feature of the tree, and therefore, it can help the tree and pot colors to coordinate esthetically. The color you choose to focus upon can be of the bark.[1] The color can also complement the color of the leaves of a tree through the summer or autumn. It can also focus on fruiting or flowering trees; the color of the pot you choose can complement the color of flowers or berries.

An example of pot structure can be taken from a sharp-cornered, rough-textured pot with strong feet. Such a pot would best suit a tree with thick-trunked pines. The dark brown/rusty texture of the pot will complement the rough bark of the coniferous tree extremely well.

POT TEXTURE

The texture of a pot is used to complement a tree as well. If the pot has smooth clay finishes, then this would be best suited for feminine trees, whereas if the pot is heavily textured, then it would bring out the masculinity and wildness of the tree. For example, if a pot is very textured with a coarse and gritty feel, then it is best suited for pines.

When selecting a pot for the bonsai, there are a multitude of factors that you would need to consider. The correct size ratio, shape, color, and texture will need to be given equal attention. However, abstract principles need to be considered that are truly unique and harmonious in nature with the bonsai.

BUYING A BONSAI POT

Now that you have an in-depth idea about selecting a pot and planting a bonsai, it is important to know where you can buy it from. Well, bonsai pots are available at local nurseries, thrift stores, pottery places, and online selling apps. You could also make your own pot.

Making Your Own pot

If you take pride in your craft, making your own bonsai pot will enthral you.[2] To move forward, you will need wood, a hammer, nails, clay, and a plastic container kiln.

- Step 1

Decide the size of the bonsai plant. Despite being the art of miniaturization, various sizes of bonsai plants exist. There exist many different types of bonsai. While making the pot, you will need to ensure that the size is appropriate to the amount of space that would be required by the roots.

Another crucial element you should remember is that the bonsai pot needs to be wide so branches can quickly spread out.

- Step 2

Using the kiln and clay, you can make a bonsai ceramic pot. A common misconception regarding bonsai pots is that they are ceramic pots with a singular hole in their base. However, that is not completely true.

A substitute that can be adopted for bonsai trees is plastic pots. Bonsai pots do not all have a single hole, nor are all of them made up of ceramic. What one chooses for their bonsai pot depends upon why they are crafting it and the available tools.

These are especially viable for trees in training. Plastic pots are cheaper, durable, and almost unbreakable.

- Step 3

You can simply use wood, a hammer, and nails to assemble a shallow bonsai pot. Cut off a few pieces of wood per your bonsai pot's decided length and width. This will make an attractive pot. Next, you would need to line the interior of the shallow wood box with plastic.

Moreover, poke small holes in the bottom of the base. You could also put a shallow plastic bowl in a wooden box. Just try to ensure it is not as tall as the wood itself. In that manner, it will not be visible.

- Step 4

Now it's time to decorate the bonsai pot. You can choose to use an old plastic bowl for this purpose, or you could get a good bowl, clean it and let it dry. Afterward, you could coat the bowl with crafter glue. You can also choose to apply any sort of surface to make the pot look attractive in appearance. You could coat it with different gels, paints, sand, and decorative items as well.

Now that you have a sufficient idea about cultivating the bonsai plant and how to make your own pot, it's time to walk through the details of a necessary evil, the drainage holes.

DRAINAGE HOLES IN THE POT

Drainage holes are a practical necessity for bonsai plants. These are important because, without them, the plant will grow in a constrained environment. Proper drainage is an essential part of preventing roots from rotting.[3]

Traditional bonsai containers usually have at least one drainage hole. Still, it is recommended to have at least two to four. You could also drill some yourself in order to ensure proper aeration.

Wiring holes

Drainage holes can moonlight as wiring holes for extremely heavy or precariously angled trees. One can choose to weave the wire through the holes and drainage mesh while affixing it to the roots of the bonsai tree. This will help the tree to stand upright in the soil.

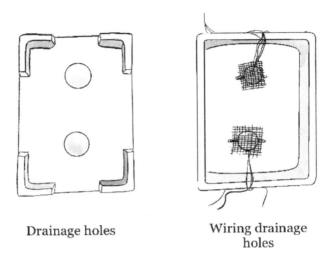

Drainage holes   Wiring drainage
holes

Importance of Drainage Holes

Among the various kinds of pots available for bonsai, there are two main types. One that is narrow and one that is shallow. However, both these types of pot have one element in common.[4] Both have a drainage facility that helps the roots grow and stay healthy.

Drainage holes are a necessary evil for bonsai plants. It's evil because, of course, the trees/plants tend to lose a lot of water. However, it is also necessary because drainage allows for aeration, root growth, and improved root health.

Drainage holes can be avoided only by those who have ample time to care for their bonsai trees. In some rare cases, where a bonsai enthusiast believes they can take care of the nutritional needs of bonsai, it is possible to avoid the holes but not recommended.

Keep in mind that bonsai trees absolutely need drainage holes, but for bonsai plants, it is not a necessity. However, giving great attention to plants that grow without drainage holes is highly recommended.

These are considered pivotal for the growth of plants, and drainage holes are significant for aeration within a pot. Drainage holes in a bonsai pot play an essential role as these decide the lifespan of a tree.

So, how does one decide the number of drainage holes in a bonsai pot? Well, the number depends on the type of tree that is grown in the pot.

Bonsai trees tend to have a fragile root system following root pruning, so bonsai soil should be able to keep the roots healthy. Roots often need to absorb air from the soil and require nitrogen to grow; as a result, aeration is provided by these holes.

SALT BUILDUP IN POTS

Among the various advantages of having holes in a bonsai pot, it is necessary to remember that these holes help avoid salt buildup. The point you should consider is that using a terra-cotta or ceramic plant pot for the bonsai, without a drainage hole, can lead to excessive salt buildup. This, as a result, leads to an unhealthy environment for the plant. As a result of which, the plant dies relatively quickly.

PREVENTION OF SOIL DRAINAGE

Soil erosion through holes in the bonsai pots is one of the significant problems bonsai hobbyists face, and there are several ways to prevent it. Some bonsai growers prefer using a plastic net to cover the drainage hole before adding soil to the pot. As bonsai trees try to grow their roots through the holes, the net will prevent that from happening.

Some options that can be utilized to prevent soil drainage include:

Covering the Holes with Liners

This technique requires planning ahead of time. Before adding soil to the pot, something must be added that would allow the water to seep out but the soil to stay.[5]

Using a Filter to Cover Holes

Contrary to popular beliefs of the past, this method is no longer considered ideal. It is now believed that adding gravel to the bottom of the pot adds to water saturation and, as a result, rot. It is recommended that one use a single large pebble instead.

Another popular method through which the hole can be covered is a broken terracotta pot. This has a curved shape and keeps the soil well-drained. It is one of a kind and ideal for bonsai pots.

Another option is to use folded coffee filters or pieces of newspaper. Although, these eventually break down and require replacement. Landscape fabric liners also perform the same function as coffee filters or newspapers. Still, they tend to last longer since they do not break down like paper.

A mesh screen can also be cut and fitted to the bottom of the pot. A plastic mesh works best as a filter—metal mesh, on the contrary, can rust.

Packing peanuts also allows for good drainage and helps keep the soil inside. These also make the pot light and do not require much soil. You could also choose to cut Styrofoam to match the shape of the plant's base. It allows the water to be drained out while keeping the soil intact.

Other ideal pot liners include coco fibres or sphagnum moss. These are particularly ideal for hanging baskets. These do a great job of keeping the soil inside the pot moist. This form of liner also works best with hanging baskets.

Recyclable Microwavable Trays for Drainage Holes

If the pot you currently use is quite large, you can use trays from microwaveable frozen meal containers. This neat trick uses something we usually throw away, considering it useless. However, the curved sides of this strainer in containers make it an ideal fit to cover drainage holes in pots while keeping the soil intact.

For larger pots, another ideal option is to use trays that steam veggies quickly. Just pushing one snugly into the bottom of the pot will provide an adequate manner to keep the soil inside. Not to forget, the container's width will also help you save money on soil.

BONSAI DRIP TRAYS

Drip tray with gravel

Another option to cover drainage holes is the bonsai drip tray. The drip trays help in protecting the surface of furniture and windowsills as excessive water drains from the bonsai. In some instances, bonsai drip trays can also be filled with water.[6] As a result, it can lead to the formation of a constantly humid environment that would lead to less transpiration.

The ideal bonsai drip trays for ceramic pots are usually thirty centimeters long. In contrast, it is ideal to have a rectangular tray that is fifty centimeters for plastic pots and larger bonsai pots. In cases where the bonsai being nurtured is subtropical in nature and requires high humidity, the drip tray can be filled with pumice gravel and water. This will create a humid environment for the bonsai tree and look decorative.

Now that we have come to the end of another chapter, you are better prepared to take over the world of bonsai cultivation. In the next chapter, to further equip you, we will walk through some handy tools that can help take care of the bonsai plant. These tools are viable and can serve the purpose of styling and nurturing.

4

TOOLS YOU NEED

In this chapter, we will walk through the tools you need to modify your bonsai plant. In order to nurture it towards growth, esthetic, and beauty, you will need to put in the time and effort.

The tools to be used are Japanese bonsai tools that are known for their high quality. Most of these tools are made of black steel and carbon steel. The difference between the two is that carbon steel tends to corrode quickly because it is galvanized during manufacturing. Black steel, however, has high strength and requires less maintenance. Tools made up of high-quality stainless steel tend to be more expensive.

In order to maintain the quality of the tools for long periods, they must be cared for extremely well. In this manner, the tool will be protected.

For ease of understanding, the tools have been divided based on their function. These are cutting tools, maintenance tools, and repotting tools.

CUTTING TOOLS

Shears and Pliers

Shears are available in a variety of shapes and sizes. These are to be used to cut twigs, smaller branches, leaves, or roots. Depending on the size of your bonsai tree collection, the shear size will vary.[1]

If most of the bonsai you have are extremely small, then there is no need to buy large shears or pliers. Shears with wide standard shapes are ideal for thicker twigs, while those with narrow and long shapes are to be used in the dense canopy.

Small shears are ideal for use if one has shohin bonsai or azaleas that need to be trimmed. Moreover, small shears can be used to remove wilted flowers as well.

Concave cutters are available with straight blades and semi-round blades. These are used to remove branches from the trunk, ideally where one wants to achieve deepened cuts that will heal without a scar. Other forms include knob cutters that leave a deepened cut. These forms of pliers are available in different sizes as well.

Cutting Tools

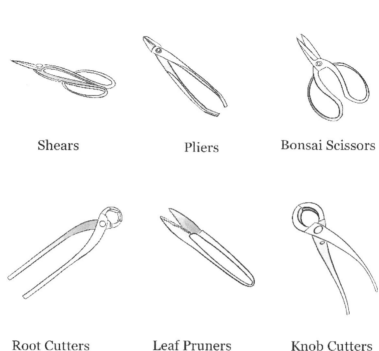

Shears   Pliers   Bonsai Scissors

Root Cutters   Leaf Pruners   Knob Cutters

Bonsai Scissors

For trees, there exist two types of scissors.

- Sturdy scissors which are long-handled and easy to grip. These are used to cut thick and fibrous roots.
- Keep in mind that to obtain neat cuts, it's important to use sharp scissors. Small pruning scissors with large handles are ideally used to trim fine twigs and smaller branches. Since these scissors have a perfect holding place, they can be used to cut shoots, fine roots, and

tiny branches as well. Alternatively, one can use a sharp surgical scissors as well.

Root Cutters

These are advanced forms of branch cutters and look almost alike. Root cutters are used to cut soil-covered roots while repotting. Additionally, it can be used as a concave branch cutter. Apart from suitably trimming and grooming the roots, root cutters are also used to reduce the size of branch stubs.

Leaf Pruner

These are also known as "pruning shears for buds and leaves." A leaf pruner has a very sharp blade and a pointed tip. It is an ideal piece of equipment for pruning dense foliage like that in maple trees.

Moreover, it is also used to cut twigs, shoots, and leaf stalks. While using shears, always avoid holding the handles of pruners sideways. Do not try to bend or twist pruners during pruning because this may damage the branch and blades.

Knob Cutters

This tool has a spherical cutting blade along with a particular use. This helps gouge out cut branches, including cases of fresh deadwood work. Once a bonsai tree has been carefully hollowed out after a cut, it can gradually achieve the desired shape.

During the process, keep in mind that working with deadwood is a very specific process. There are a multitude of tools and knives that can be used for this purpose so as to make the deadwood look as natural as possible.

TOOLS FOR WIRING

To wire a bonsai tree, one needs to have wire in various diameters, wire cutters, and pliers to bend the wire. These tools are available in different shapes and sizes. If a person has numerous shohin bonsai, they must have small pruners. The wire used for bonsai is made of annealed aluminum or copper. It is often suggested that beginners use aluminum, as it is easy to apply.

Wire Cutters

In order to shape and train the bonsai tree, wires are used. Wire cutters or scissors are used to cut these wires. The small scissors come in handy when trimming the wire ends while wiring secondary branches. Normally there are two kinds of wire cutters that are used. Cutters are to be selected as per the size of the wire. A general wire cutter is used to cut aluminum wires. It is the ideal equipment when wire needs to be cut in tight spots. A heavy-duty wire cutter is ideal when cutting copper wires and thicker gauges.

Tools for Wiring

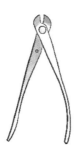  

| Wire Cutters | Concave Branch Cutters | Bonsai Saw |

Branch Cutters

Normally there are three types of branch cutters available. Branch cutters are generally used to cut thinner, pencil-thickness branches, mostly for deciduous trees and thin conifers. Concave branch cutters, on the contrary, have a curved cutting edge. These are used to trim branch stubs close to the trunk. These are also utilized when wood needs to be peeled. A flat branch cutter has a flat edge and serves the same function as a pruner. It is used to cut branches neatly, especially those that are closer to the trunk. A hybrid branch cutter, on the contrary, performs the function of being both a concave and flat cutter. These are, however, a bit different to use; they usually require some practice.

The blade of the branch cutter should be used on a branch with one-third of its length. If one cuts large branches with the same cutter, there is a risk of breaking the cutting jaws of the tool.

A form of best practice is to use the rear ends of the blades to cut instead of the tip. This is because the tip of the tool is at the most risk of breaking if any twisting movement is performed while cutting the branch.

Bonsai Saw

This is a pruning saw specifically made for bonsai. This saw has a thin blade and fine teeth. It serves the function of making delicate and precise cuts in branches as it utilizes the pull stroke. A pull stroke is one in which the saw is pulled towards oneself instead of away. It provides more control and thereby prevents the shredding of delicate bark during cutting.

REPOTTING TOOLS

When you transplant a pot-bound bonsai into fresh soil, it is called repotting. This action allows entangled roots to gain space, oxygen, and nutrition from the fresh soil. Before repotting, the roots need to be reshaped and pruned. The number of times the tree will be repotted depends upon age, pot size, and other factors.[2]

Chopsticks

When you transplant a tree, bamboo chopsticks and sharp-edged metal chopsticks are used to comb the roots. However, one can also use a root hook or rake in this manner. If you are working with fine and delicate roots, then use your fingers and toothpicks.

Loppers

These normally resemble pruners, but these are also capable of cutting thick roots, branches, and trunks (over two centimeters) in contrast to pruners. Moreover, these have a strong handle for an excellent grip.

Root Claws

As the name indicates, root claws are used to comb roots for bonsai. It is used to break down large soil pieces into small pieces during repotting. One has to be extremely careful while using it. Any mishandling or excessive force during the usage of root claws can damage the roots. In case the roots are not thick, one can use a rake/hook.

Repotting tools

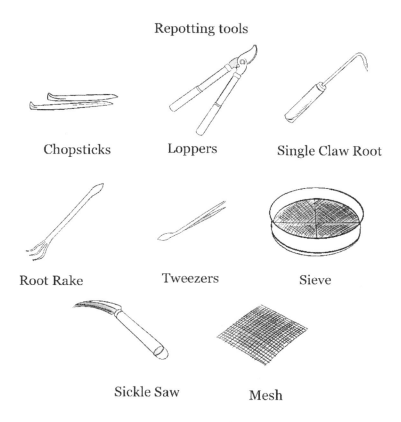

Chopsticks　　Loppers　　Single Claw Root

Root Rake　　Tweezers　　Sieve

Sickle Saw　　Mesh

Needle-Nosed Tweezers

In contrast to normal tweezers, these tweezers are multi-purpose, as they have fine tips. These gardening tweezers are used to perform tasks that require precision. Some examples of fine tasks include:

- Handling the sprouts.
- Cleaning debris after repotting
- Picking up and throwing off any bugs.
- Plucking tiny weeds and leaves.

Sieve

The sieve used for bonsai plants has larger holes to help sort through different soil particles during repotting.

Sickle Saw

Unlike the root saw, the sickle saw is slightly curved. The purpose of a sickle saw is to free the corners of a tree from the pot. In this manner, the tree can be easily removed from the pot. Instead of using a sickle saw, one can also use a root saw.

Mesh

This is a net used to cover the holes at the bottom of the pot. The mesh prevents insects from invading the soil and also prevents the soil from coming out of holes when one waters the bonsai.

ADDITIONAL TOOLS

These additional tools can be opted for once a person gains adequate knowledge about maintenance and care. The additional tools include electric tools, hand-operated tools, and heavy-duty cutters. In case one wants to practice advanced techniques like creating deadwood while styling a bonsai, these tools will make the job easier.

Rotary Tool

This tool is a carving power tool that is used to carve and cut deadwood. There are smaller and larger rotary tools. Small-sized rotary tools are great to begin working with and often fit smaller carving bits of work. One can use large and more powerful rotary tools to carve with excessive speed. It adds more flexibility to work.

Chisels and Grafting Knives

Chisels are used to split and remove wood. Moreover, it can help create jin and shari. The grafting knives serve the purpose of creating a natural look.

Scalpel

This carving tool is specific for bonsai. Knives and scalpels allow one to perform more detailed work with more control.

Additional Tools

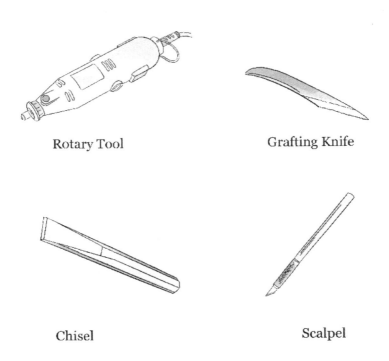

Rotary Tool

Grafting Knife

Chisel

Scalpel

MAINTENANCE TOOLS FOR BONSAI

Brushes—Soft and Wire Brush

In order to remove debris from the soil surface, a coconut or fern fiber brush is used. It is also used to clean the rotating table. A wire brush contains soft brass filaments. It is used to remove algae deposits from the surface of pots. In order to do so, it is important to lubricate the brush with water. The brushes can also be used to clean the trunk, bark, branches, and deadwood area of trees.

Wound Sealant

A wound sealant is a paste that has antibacterial and antifungal agents. It is utilized to fill the cut wounds on a bonsai tree to prevent infections and diseases.

During the process of pruning, you might make some wounds intentionally. Bear in mind that trees do not heal from the inside out; rather, they form a tissue known as a callus to heal.

Wires

The wire that is used for bonsai ranges in gauge from 0.3 to 8. Generally, an ideal wire is one-third of the thickness of the branch that is to be wired. As previously discussed, anodized aluminum is the ideal fit to shape deciduous bonsai. The wire is typically flexible and easy to use. In general, it is recommended that beginners should work with anodized aluminum wire before using copper wire. Moreover, it is important to remember that anodized aluminum is less noticeable and more esthetic.

In contrast to anodized aluminum, annealed copper is ideal for thick branches like those of conifers. This wire is harder and keeps the branches in place efficiently.

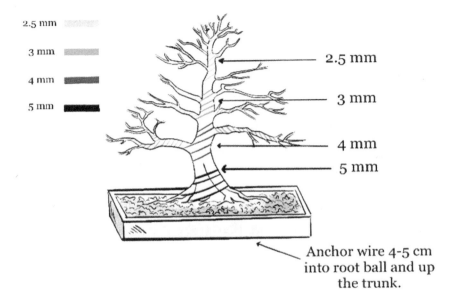

2.5 mm

3 mm

4 mm

5 mm

2.5 mm

3 mm

4 mm

5 mm

Anchor wire 4-5 cm
into root ball and up
the trunk.

Thickness of wires

Watering Can

A watering can is one of the simplest but most essential acces-
sories for bonsai care. A watering can with a long nozzle and a
small hose is ideal for watering bonsai trees and helps get water
around the pot.

Spray Bottle

One can choose to opt for a spray bottle to water the leaves and
flowers. Moreover, it can also be used to clean dirt from the pot
during repotting.

Turntable

It is fairly difficult to lift and turn heavy trees at all times. While working on the bonsai, you will turn it around quite a few times, and as a result, you may end up scratching the table the bonsai is standing on.

WHERE TO BUY TOOLS

These tools can be bought online, at hardware stores, or local nurseries.

CARE AND MAINTENANCE

So, when you finally bite the bullet and purchase a nice set of bonsai tools, you will need to maintain them. Some maintenance strategies that can be adopted to improve a bonsai's life include never using dirty tools on different trees, as it could lead to the spread of disease. Also, depending on the quality of the tools, some can get damaged if overused.

As the bonsai tools are used daily, they will definitely get dirty. Depending on the species of tree you are working on, it may also attract sap, which will lead to more dirt sticking to the tool. A sanding block eraser is one of the easiest ways to clean the tool. These work similarly to normal erasers; however, they are combined with a fine grit sandpaper without being too rough. If there is sap on the edges of your tool, you can also use a black sand eraser.

Another important factor to consider is that tools need to be used with sharp edges. Sharpening tools with curved edges using diamond-impregnated finishing stone is another maintenance strategy that one can adopt.

For pruning tools made of carbon steel, the best way to make them shiny and glossy is to use oil such as Tsubaki oil or WD-40. All one will need to do is apply or spray the oil and wipe it off immediately. Hand cleaner or rubbing alcohol works as well. This method will not only preserve the shine of the metal but also help if there is rust on the tools. If, on the contrary, you have tools made up of stainless steel, then simply wipe them since the stainless steel keeps them shiny.

Now that you have reached the end of yet another chapter, applaud yourself for the enthusiasm you have shown. On the route to creating and maintaining a bonsai plant, you now have sufficient knowledge about pots and tools.

5

HOW TO START A BONSAI

Bonsai is one of the most eminent styles of tree in the world. Credited for their esthetically pleasing miniature structure, these trees have astoundingly taken over the craft for people from all walks of life. One of the most famous bonsai is the Chinese Bird Plums (Sageretia theezans) which are a part of Penjing Landscape by Yee-sun Wu. The landscape comprises Ficus Bonsai, which makes a realistic and beautiful scenery.

Whether you are inspired by these famous bonsai, or you are a hobbyist by nature, starting a bonsai is an art in itself. In this chapter, we will walk through some of the most famous techniques of starting a bonsai. The details in this section, for these popular methods, have been kept brief because these techniques are a bit too advanced for beginners and will be covered in-depth in my next book.

Keep in mind that bonsai experts know many other techniques, but those listed here are the most popular. In the upcoming chapter, we will explore the three most popular methods of growing bonsai all around the world.

ADVANCED TECHNIQUES

Air Layering

A popular technique used in horticulture to propagate trees is air layering. The aim of air layering is to propagate trees in a vegetative manner (asexually).

Seedlings

Although bonsai tends to grow very slowly from seeds, this can be a beneficial method if you want to start from scratch. Remember, growing a bonsai takes years, and mostly, they outlive their grower, but the satisfaction you get watching them grow is definitely unmatched.

Growing from Cuttings

Cultivating trees through cuttings is popular among bonsai growers because it's an inexpensive way to get new trees.

Tanuki

Tanuki is the process in which a single bonsai is grown using two different sources of plant material. In this technique, a live bonsai is paired with deadwood.

Root-Over-Rock Style

In this style, the bonsai is attached to the rock with wires, and the tree lives entirely on the rock, growing in a special soil mix.

Grafting

Another method of growing bonsai is through grafting. The procedure can be performed to add a branch to a specific bonsai, replace foliage with a more delicate variety, or add roots.

THREE SIMPLE STRATEGIES TO START A BONSAI

Now that you know some advanced techniques, let's focus on the three most popular techniques for growing a bonsai.

#1 - Buying a Finished Bonsai in a Pot

One of the simplest strategies for starting a bonsai is to buy a finished one in a pot. However, this technique has some pros and cons attached to it. One of the significant benefits of purchasing a bonsai in a pot from a store or nursery is that various species are available to choose from.

Another two-edged advantage of buying a bonsai from a nursery or store is that the cost may vary. In some instances, you may find that the bonsai is exceptionally expensive, depending on its structure. See, the thicker a bonsai trunk is, and the more colossal the tree is, the more expensive it becomes. This notion may become hefty if you have a low budget.

Another pro associated with buying a bonsai from the store is that it is already done, pruned, wired, and shaped in a pot. All that is required is that one maintains it.

Finished Bonsai in a pot

Despite the pros of buying a bonsai in a pot, there are also some cons. One downside is that most stores sell junipers, since these are the world's most notable species of bonsai. Still, unfortunately, at a beginner's level, they are hard to maintain. Given the limited choice in stores, one may feel obligated to buy this species.

Buying a bonsai in a pot online has its cons as well. For example, if a bonsai is ordered online, there is a high probability that it will die by the time one receives it. After spending a lot of funds online in making that purchase, this seems like a significant drawback.

When buying a bonsai in a pot, enthusiasts often question the pricing. The expensive nature of a bonsai in a pot is that an individual has spent time and effort growing it thus far. The high cost is synonymous with the time and energy spent in growing it perfectly.

The cost of bonsai may also differ depending on the type of pot. These can be Chinese pots which are relatively cheaper and ideal for beginners.

When deciding upon which species to buy, it is essential to keep note of the plant's journey. In other words, understand which stage of life the plant is currently in.

Moreover, deciding on the plant's location is crucial before buying it. If it is going to be kept indoors, then Carmona, the ficus, jade tree, and Chinese elm would be ideal. Popular outdoor bonsai that you could choose from include pine, juniper, and maple.

Indoor bonsai trees can be found widely in home improvement stores and online shops. When finding a bonsai in a pot, these aforementioned species of plants may be four to five years old, which is relatively young by bonsai standards. Keep in mind indoor bonsai can be a bit expensive because they are imported from large nurseries in China.

If the idea of buying a bonsai from stores seems expensive, then you can explore other methods as well. More often than not, people don't even buy a bonsai. They are usually given one as either a gift or inheritance. The individuals then focus on maintaining it from there on.

#2 – Dig a Tree from the Ground

Compared to buying a bonsai from a nursery or store, digging it from the ground is a better option. A tree dug from the ground is mature material and an excellent option for bonsai enthusiasts.

Some trees have extraordinary qualities for bonsai growth. As a result, dig them out directly and plant them in a pot. Before learning about the steps to digging a tree out, remember that it is illegal to do so in national forests, state or government land. Moreover, if you plan to dig it out from someone else's property, you will need to get their permission.

To find good garden material, you could search online or go to your local hardware store or nursery. The ideal time to dig out bonsai is during early spring, so inquiring about these tools prior to the season is a good choice.

Among the various options available for digging, some ideal choices include azalea, yew, privet, lonicera, and hornbeam. These species are ideal cases for transplantation. Try to look for large shrubby plants to dig out.

As a rule of thumb, every meter of branch length will facilitate the creation of a thickness of almost one centimeter. If you manage to find a plant with several branches of multiple meters, then it will lead to the creation of a decent trunk. If you select a shrub with few low branches, then chances are that you can easily trim away and create a tapered trunk.

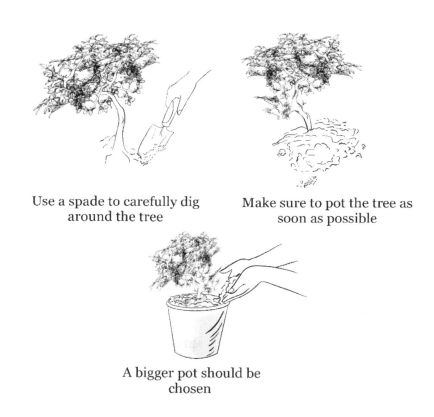

Use a spade to carefully dig
around the tree

Make sure to pot the tree as
soon as possible

A bigger pot should be
chosen

The step-by-step plan for digging out a tree is as follows:

1. Firstly, dig around the tree using a spade, being very careful to not damage the root system around it.
2. Then carefully lift the tree up and place it on slightly moist sheets. Then wrap the sheets around the root system of the tree to prevent the tree from drying out.

Remember to pot the tree as soon as you get back home.

3. From the place you dig out the tree, collect some soil mixture and, using it, prepare one for your plant.

4. Before planting the tree in a pot, remember to choose a large pot with a drainage hole. Fill it up with almost ¼ mixture of gravel and akadama in a ratio of 1:1

5. Before potting, carefully unwrap the sheets from the root system and place the tree delicately in the pot. Then fill in the empty spaces at the sides using the originally collected soil mixture mixed with akadama, at a ratio of 1:1

6. Finally, rinse a considerable amount of water on the tree, while being careful not to disturb the soil surface, using a fine nozzle.

COLLECTING A SHRUB FOR BONSAI

If you are considering digging shrubs for a bonsai, the steps may vary slightly. Before setting off on your journey, remember to prepare a few things, like ensuring that there is a sufficient substrate and a range of pot sizes available at home. Another good option is to have a stack of wood that can be used to build a fitting grow box. Remember to plant the shrub as soon as it is dug up.

Before digging shrubs in someone else's garden, remember that most owners dislike a mess. In such a case scenario, it is ideal to discuss the plan beforehand and make any payments ahead of time.

1. Trim the shrub to a manageable size using a large caliper branch lopper. Keep to the required size because larger branches protect buds in critical places during transportation.

2. Using a sharp blade, cut a circle around the trunk between ten to thirty centimeters away from the trunk. Usually, this will provide you with a good root ball, making transportation easier.

3. The soil outside the circle is removed on one side of the tree to make an undercut in the root ball.

4. While lifting the tree, remember that soft sandy soil often easily drops from the roots. In this regard, it is essential to ensure that a bag or cloth is nearby and the soil is moist. Wrap the root ball immediately with the cloth. This will allow the roots to be protected.

5. When you reach home, clean off the soil with a root hook. This will gently but swiftly remove the soil. Try to work in a shaded space, out of the wind, and spray water if required.

6. Once the soil has been cleaned, you can see the optimal nebari. Choose the nebari line based on the smallest cuts required.

7. Trim the roots back as far as possible. This is typically back to the root's first branching, leaving the smaller branches and trimming the main root.

8. Now it will be possible for you to decide the size of the final tree and cut the branches back to a rough outline.

9. Then put a layer of substrate in the pot, wiggle the tree in place, and tie the tree down within the pot.

10. If the roots are weak, then tie them to branches. Fixing the plant properly allows for recovery and reduces the risk of having the tree blown out of the pot during the initial establishment period.

11. Ensure that the nebari is covered with a few centimeters of the substrate. This will allow for the development of new roots.

#3 - Buying a Tree from a Local Nursery or Hardware Store

In the world of bonsai art, another popular and preferred method is to buy a tree from a local nursery or hardware store. The advantage of this technique is that it is inexpensive in nature. On the flip side, however, working on an old tree means that one must remove large branches with visible wounds.

Shrubs from a nursery

An ideal place to buy would be family-owned nurseries. The principal aspects you should keep note of include.[1]

- Paying close attention to plants that seem healthy and hydrated.
- Try to stick to the commonly recommended species of bonsai
- Don't overlook the clearance table
- Look for plants that are well-branched with symmetry, balance, and proportion.
- Choose a bonsai that is beautiful to you
- Select plants with healthy foliage

REPOTTING BONSAI

In time, after you have started your bonsai, you will need to repot it. Slowly and gradually, as your bonsai grows, the roots system will become more crowded and take up more room in the pot. This will make it difficult for the plant to get enough oxygen or nutrients. Therefore it is necessary to repot the bonsai.

Repotting is usually done in spring, at the beginning of vegetation. The timings vary for each species, for example;

- Every three to five years for conifers;
- Every two to three years for deciduous trees;
- Every one or two years for fruit trees;
- Every two years for indoor bonsai trees.

In this regard, it is important to remember that different tree species require repotting at slightly different times. Different trees of the same species can be repotted at slightly different times, even those grown in exactly the same climate.

THE IDEAL TIME FOR REPOTTING

Repotting should not be done routinely but only when it is absolutely necessary. The time can vary depending on the species of the bonsai, the age, the size of the original pot, and growing conditions.

Generally, younger trees need repotting every two years, whereas older trees need it every three to five years. The key indicator for repotting is the root of the bonsai; when the root circles around the root system, the plant needs repotting.

HOW TO REPOT

The following steps can be undertaken to repot a bonsai.

- Using a root hook, remove the bonsai tree from the pot. Look at the roots and their formation level to decide if it needs repotting.
- Using a chopstick, tease out the old compost, regardless of whether repotting is required or not. Ensure that this step is done carefully; it is also crucial to trim the roots that are too long.

- If planting in a new pot, the drainage holes should be covered with mesh to prevent the new, loose soil from falling through.
- If the bonsai does not need repotting, choose a new pot that is the same height as the width of the ground root. This is normally one- to two-thirds of the tree height.
- Place a layer of soil at the bottom of the pot.
- Once a nice layer of the growing medium has been established, add more of it around the tree.
- Water the tree thoroughly; within a couple of weeks, a beautiful tree will have grown.

TOOLS TO REPOT

Some standard tools include a root rake, which will help loosen the root and soil from the pot. Scissors to trim the roots before repotting. Chopstick or any long flat wooden stick that will entice the clumped-up soil to loosen and fall off the roots.[2]

LOCATION OF THE BONSAI

While growing a bonsai, it is important to remember that it it also requires sunlight. Depending on its location, bonsai can be indoor or outdoor in nature.

Indoor Bonsai

A bonsai tree can be placed inside or outside depending on its species and your preference. In-house bonsai usually do well when there is a south-facing window, since a lot of sunlight is crucial for bonsai. Usually, indoor bonsai are subtropical species like the ficus or Carmona. These trees need relative humidity around them to grow. Some popular indoor bonsai include the dwarf jade, the Fukien tea (Carmona), the Hawaiian umbrella (Schefflera), and the sweet plum (Sageretia).[3]

Outdoor Bonsai

Depending on your location, most outdoor trees will need to be placed outside year-round. The annual cycle is crucial for the health of most trees. As a rule of thumb, bonsai trees must be placed outside in a bright spot.[4] If a person's location is extremely hot, then afternoon shade can be beneficial for the trees.

GROWING A BONSAI WITH LITTLE TO NO SUN

Some species of trees can withstand cold weather. These do not need direct sunlight and do better in cold, damp environments. Generally, bonsai trees need different amounts of sunlight depending on their species. However, typically most of the eminent species require full sunlight.

GROWING A BONSAI INDOORS

Most bonsai hobbyists find it ideal to treat their bonsai as a houseplant. In such a scenario, it is important to remember that the tree can be grown inside the house.

Keep in mind, as a general rule, bonsai trees require 100 percent humidity to survive. However, most homes do not have a humidity-rich environment. Heating and air-conditioning systems may cause the bonsai soil to dry. To counter this issue, a humid tray can be placed on the tree, or the bonsai can be misted frequently.

FAST FORWARDING THE GROWTH OF BONSAI

An average bonsai tree takes almost three to five years before it begins to look like a little tree. After that time, the tree grows twelve to eighteen inches in a year. Full maturity for the bonsai is usually reached at approximately ten to twelve years, but some species can grow twelve to thirty-six inches per year and reach maturity within the first three years of their life.

FACTORS INFLUENCING GROWTH

Several factors may influence the growth rate of a bonsai tree. These include the species of bonsai, the growing conditions, pruning, and the age of the tree.

Fast Growers

If you are currently in search of a fast-growing tree, then you could choose the Chinese elm, the maple, the ficus, or the various pine trees. All of these trees grow twelve to thirty-six inches in a year. This growth rate also influences the time it takes bonsai to reach maturity. This usually happens in about the first three years.

Average Growers

The two most popular bonsai trees, juniper and cotoneaster, depict an average growth rate. Their average annual growth rate is five to twelve inches per year and they reach maturity in the first four years of their life.

Slow Growers

The trees that are the slowest growers include jades, Fukien trees, wisterias and azaleas. These grow only two to five inches in a year and reach maturity once they reach five years.

TIPS TO GROW FAST

If you want to expedite the growth process for the bonsai, then the following tips will help:

- Place the bonsai tree in an area that receives ample sunlight for four hours daily.
- Water the bonsai tree every day until the soil is moist to the touch.
- Fertilize the bonsai plant every three weeks during the growing season. This is from early spring to mid-fall in most regions. Follow the dilution instructions robustly; otherwise, there is a risk of burning the bonsai roots.
- Repot the bonsai every two years in the spring before the growing cycle. During replanting, trim at least a third of the roots from the end.

- Check the bonsai plant for pest infestations. If present, treat with a small dose of pesticide.

If you are a bonsai hobbyist with a time crunch, then an ideal choice would be to choose a fast-growing bonsai species. Fast-growing bonsai is great because it is significantly easier to shape and train them.

Several fast-growing tree types exist today; these include deciduous, evergreen, coniferous, and succulent trees. The versatile nature of these trees allows the bonsai gardener to choose from trees that would bear flowers and leaves or portray various colors and unique shapes.

6

WATERING A BONSAI

Now that you have sufficient knowledge about growing a bonsai, we shall walk through another important element of plant survival, watering. After all, plants cannot survive without water, and the correct way to do so is often neglected.

QUANTITY OF WATER FOR A BONSAI

Mostly, bonsai are watered once their caretaker feels that the moisture in the soil is relatively low. The confusing part is, however, the quantity of water required. The amount you would need for a bonsai depends on the species, similar to the time of watering.

A good rule of thumb is to water the plant enough to soak the tree's entire root system. There are two common methods of soaking the roots. These are overhead watering and watering by immersion. Overhead watering is basically when a bonsai is showered using a hose or watering can, using a fine spray only, until water is leaking out of the drainage holes.

On the other hand, immersion is a quick method for the roots of the bonsai to soak in the water. This method is ideal for indoor trees or those that have dried out. However, it is important to remember that immersion can often start damaging the roots.

One major reason why immersing can be damaging to the roots is the fact that "over-watering" is an actual phenomenon. In order to avoid over-watering a bonsai, it is vital to check the soil moisture. The soil should be moist at all times but not wet. The period between watering allows oxygen to reach the roots, thereby promoting growth. If the soil is constantly soaked, this process cannot occur.

Some symptoms of over-watering that one should look out for include an unstable trunk, branches that are weak or small, a change in leaf color, and leaf drop. Changes like these indicate that the tree has been over-watered for some time, and there is a substantial risk of root rot.

FINGER METHOD

A simple way of determining whether your bonsai needs to be watered is the finger method. In order to do this, just gently press the tip of your finger an inch down within the soil and leave it there for about twenty seconds. This will allow you to gain a good sense of how damp the soil is. If you find that the top inch of the soil is dry to the touch, then go ahead and water it.

WHEN IS THE BEST TIME TO WATER?

The ideal time to water a bonsai is when the soil starts feeling dry. There is no particular rule about the time associated with watering a bonsai. Just remember to avoid watering it through during the afternoon with cold water because the soil is already warmed up by sunlight and will cool down quickly.

Another crucial point to remember is that bonsai do not need to be watered when the soil is wet. Just water the soil when it feels and looks dry. Remember that the soil should never become "completely" dry.

There should never be a routine schedule to water the bonsai. Some factors that should be exclusively focused on include season, tree species, and climate.

Season

The watering needs for a bonsai are heavily dependent upon the season. However, keep in mind that it changes much slower than the weather. In the month of October, there are days when large pots do not need to be watered daily.

In northern European countries, it tends to rain throughout November. In such scenarios, it is ideal to put trees in the shade so they do not get excessively wet.

Watering can be paused for weeks during the overwintering season for bonsai in a greenhouse or foil tent. Usually, plants are not watered until the beginning of February. In the tent or greenhouse, the humidity is often so high that there is hardly a need for watering.

Climate

The climatic conditions have an influence on the watering needs for bonsai. For example, winter in northern Sweden and summer in southern Greece require more attention to watering than in temperate areas.

Tree species

In between different tree species, the water requirements tend to vary. The different species have been created by adapting to different conditions in their natural location. For example, an olive bonsai adapted to southern Spain has different demands for water supply than a ficus bonsai from rainy subtropics.

Some trees tend to be particularly thirsty in nature; these include redwood bonsai, hornbeam bonsai, and larch bonsai. These species require extra care in midsummer. It is ideal to place them in the shade, especially in the afternoon. In the case of these species, having an automatic sprinkler system installed is also a good option.

THE CORRECT WAY TO WATER TREES

The best way bonsai trees can be watered is the "soak and dry" method. In this method, first, you would have to soak the soil completely and then allow the soil to dry out completely. Ensure the bonsai trees are in well-draining soil in a pot with drainage holes.

In the case of indoor bonsai, it is better that the water does not sit on top of the leaves. If the water is allowed to sit on the leaves for too long, it can lead to the rotting of roots. In the case of outdoor bonsai, this is not much of an issue because there is ample airflow, and water tends to dry quicker.

WATERING FOR INDOOR AND OUTDOOR TREES

The most important rule for watering trees is to never water on routine. All one needs to do is monitor for when the need arises. Watering could be required every three days or several times a day. It really depends on the weather, size, and species.

With the watering of bonsai, it is essential to remember that humidity plays an important role in the equation. All Proflowers bonsais are equipped with humidity trays and a bag of pebbles. Once the humidity tray has been uncovered, be sure to place the pebbles in it to increase the humidity level for the tree.

WATER CARE ON HOT DAYS

Climate change today has drastically influenced every living being in the world. In these times, it is crucial to adopt newer and better strategies. In the long run, these protective strategies will be the stepping stones for bonsai's growth.

1. Move the tree to a climate-controlled area

If the area you currently reside in sees high summers, it would be a good idea to move the bonsai indoors or into a greenhouse. If this is not possible, try to provide some shade for the plant.

2. Water the bonsai

If the bonsai you are nurturing is placed outdoors, then over-watering it is impossible. In times like these, the plant can use every drop of water it can get. During the summer, a soil moisture meter is a good option.

3. Fine spray misting

In summer, it is a good idea to keep the leaves hydrated along with the soil; however, the downside is the possibility of the droplets sticking to the leaves. So, a better option is to use sprays with a fine mist to ensure that droplets do not stick to the leaves. In this position, they will act as magnifying glasses that burn the leaves.

4. Avoid nitrogen-heavy fertilizers

Nitrogen fertilizers in large quantities are harsh on the soil. However, in summer, the intensity of their impact increases by notches. A better alternative is organic fertilizer, like a compost-based product or fertilizer blend that has been explicitly made for bonsai.

5. Right water cans

Watering is an essential function for bonsai plants. Self-watering planters are designed to wick up water from the water reservoir at the bottom of the planter. If these are correctly set with the wick inserted deep enough, one will not have to worry about watering the soil.

Among different watering cans, the most critical difference is the one that exists between the length and shape of the spout. A standard-sized spout is ideal for all-purpose watering and fertilizing.

A brass rose spout, sometimes also called a rosette, works best when one wants to mimic a soft rain shower which is what the bonsai are accustomed to, and it helps them thrive.

Now that you have a better idea about how you can water and cater to the needs of bonsai, it is time to move towards pruning. In the next chapter, we will walk through the different methods you can use to effectively prune the trees.

7

PRUNING PRIORITIES

Throughout the process of growing a bonsai, one has to prune it thoroughly to style it and shape it to the desired form. The core reason behind pruning is that trees tend to concentrate most growth on the top and outer parts of the stem. In this light, these growth areas must be pruned to encourage growth towards the inner parts of the tree.

There exist two forms of pruning: maintenance pruning and structural or stylistic pruning. The maintenance form of pruning keeps the tree small and encourages its growth. The structural one shapes the tree and is a form of art.

Before embarking on the journey to prune your bonsai, you will need a critical eye and bonsai batch or knob cutters. To help navigate your way, in this chapter, we will walk through branch selection and the best time to prune.

BEST SEASON TO PRUNE

Generally, the best time to prune a tree is during early spring and, in some cases, late autumn, just before and after the growing season. The exact time which is ideal for pruning differs from species to species. For example, a ficus bonsai has a different pruning time than juniper bonsai.

One form of pruning is winter pruning, in which deciduous trees are pruned in their dormancy period. The time begins at the end of autumn and lasts up until the beginning of spring. It is an outstanding opportunity to take a good look at broadleaf trees while they are clear of obscuring foliage. Moreover, one can take this time to set up their trees for the year ahead.

WINTER PRUNING OF DECIDUOUS TREES

The main actions that are taken while pruning deciduous trees include:

- Removing crossing branches
- Removing branches that grow directly up or down
- Remove large buds present at the tips of branches
- Thin out the number of branches from busy areas of the tree
- Imagining it beforehand

Before you prune, envision what you want to achieve with the side in front of you.

BRANCH SELECTION

Throughout the bonsai pruning process, one will encounter experiences in which a branch will have to be selected. This is important for the purpose of creating deadwood and sometimes for the purpose of esthetics as well.

Depending on the branch's position, one will either wire it, remove it, or prune it. In this section of the chapter, we will walk through the various kinds of branches that you may encounter.

Branches within the Lower One-Third of the Tree

Branches that are present in this position should definitely be removed so as to show the trunk line. This will allow the exposure of nebari and a clear view of the bottom part of the trunk.

Branch removal   Exposed trunk

An exception for these branches may exist in which a person leaves them as sacrifice branches to help with the thickening of the lower trunk.

Bar Branches

These branches originate at the same level as other branches. If these are present in direct opposition to each other, these are known as bar branches. Another issue that one may encounter is that if there are too many branches originating at more or less the same point, there will be a lot of sap flow through the area, leading to an unsightly thickening of that area. This would also lead to reverse taper. In the case of bar branches, a better option is to remove as many as possible, especially those found in pines where the branches form a whorl. A preferable scheme is to leave the opposite branch system.

Parallel Branches

These branches usually originate close but are present directly above each other. These are more directed toward esthetics. A good guideline to keep in mind is the classical design for these. For this pattern, you would keep a branch to one side, the next up on the other side, and then a back branch repeated alongside. Keep in mind this is an ideal and not always possible design.

Branches That Grow from Almost the Same Point

These branches do not necessarily grow parallel above each other or from the same height; rather, these are just close enough to be unsightly separate. There is also a possibility that this will lead to a situation where the area can thicken disproportionately compared to where other branches grow to increase the sap flow.

Vigorously Growing Branches

These branches tend to take energy away from other branches and can cast a shadow across other branches due to their fast growth. It is also possible that these branches will thicken disproportionately to other branches and interfere with normal taper or the notion that branches lower down the trunk should be thicker than branches that are present high up the trunk. These branches need to be shortened or removed.

The Leader

Old trees tend to show a rounder apex, which can be achieved by removing the leader and substituting it with a new leader or wiring it in a manner that provides a more rounded form. This action also helps reduce apical dominance and redistribute the energy in a tree.

SHAVING THE BARK OF BONSAI

More often than not, deadwood is created to improve the esthetic of a bonsai. The creation of deadwood on bonsai in the form of Jin, Shari, or Uro can enhance the tree's character significantly. A "Jin" is a bare-stripped part of a branch, a "Shari" is a barkless part of the trunk, and an "Uro" is a hollow, irregularly shaped wound in the trunk.

Deadwood

In order to create deadwood, the bark of the bonsai is shaved. For example, if a flaky juniper is stripped of the old, dead, flaky bark, the dark red bark underneath can be revealed. It is beautiful esthetic-wise and can be made better by applying vegetable oil.

The best time to shave the bark of a tree to create deadwood is in the early spring or later summer because the tree will heal the wounds relatively quickly.

CUT PASTE

Bonsai cut paste is a thick, clay-based sealant used to seal the cuts and keep sap from bleeding. Cut paste is used by kneading it in the form of a ball, then flattening it between fingers before applying it to the bonsai wound.

The purpose of having a cut paste is to control how the scar tissue forms and looks after healing. It is also extremely useful to prevent the tree section from dying when a full trunk cut or large branch cut has been made.[1]

Now that you know the best time to prune and the elements to consider during branch selection, it is time to learn more about shaping and wiring. In the next chapter, we will discuss the techniques for creating the desired style.

One of the most pivotal aspects of caring for a bonsai is the fact that it can be shaped into any shape. Bonsai hobbyists often prefer "bending" the branches of a bonsai to create a particular look.

This feature associated with bonsai is demonstrated by one of the most famous displays in the world. It was known as Mame

Bonsai Display by Morten Albek. The display has a bonsai, a scroll, and an accent plant.

Together, these objects create a powerful image and often denote the celebration of the current season. If you want to craft something up to the standards of these eminent displays, then follow the route of bending and shaping a bonsai.

8

SHAPING AND WIRING

WHY BEND AND SHAPE BONSAI?

A common misconception in many minds is that bonsai trees are just small species. In truth, although they are miniature in nature, bonsai hold the capability of being propagated like any other tree. All a bonsai requires is training and shaping effects. The wiring of the tree is necessary because it allows it to be molded as per the desired form. Wiring the bonsai allows the tree to be guided in growth even in unnatural methods like shakan slanting form.

WHICH DIRECTION TO WIRE?

In the beginning, one should always try to fix a singular end of the bonsai wire within the ground or the branch. Fixing within the ground means simply placing the end of the wire, which is four to five centimeters, into the ground. The preferred location is behind the tree. The direction of the wire is either from the bottom towards the top or from inside to outside. In essence, it always moves from a stronger to a weaker point. The wire can move clockwise or counter clockwise, depending on the direction you plan to bend.

Wrap the wire tightly without excessive pressure. If the wire is wrapped loosely, it will not hold the position of the branch after bending. Work your way towards the thickest branches and then to the thinnest. Bend the wire up the truck and outwards on the branches from the trunk to the tip. Your position should be such that the wire is facing you. The wire has to be wrapped around the limbs at a 45-degree angle in a "barber pole" style. The wire should conform to the limb and guide its direction, but it should not be over-tightened. Keep in mind that the plant is growing and will need space.

45 degree angle

Too loose

WIRING METHODS

There are two major techniques through which a bonsai can be wired. These are single and double wiring methods. In double-wiring methods, two branches of similar thickness are wired near each other using a single piece of wire. The remaining branches are wired separately using single wiring. It is essential to wire all the branches intended for shaping before bending them.

Single Wiring

Like double wiring, one has to ensure enough wire to wrap around the trunk twice. The wire length and thickness should also be enough to be wrapped at a 45-degree angle. If you apply multiple wires to the same part of the trunk or branch, it is important to place them neatly together without crossing them.

Double Wiring

In order to double wire a bonsai, select the pair of branches that need to be wired. The branches selected should have the same level of thickness and should be available near each other on the trunk. Remember, the wire should wrap around the trunk preferably twice so as to not move when bending the branches later on.

Next, cut the right length of wire for both branches. Then wrap the wire through the trunk and upon one branch at a time.

Make sure that the wire is wrapped from the base of the branch to the very tip before moving to other branches. The wire should be wrapped around the branch at 45 degrees to make the tree grow thicker.

Once all suitable branches have been wired, the rest can be wired with a simple-wiring technique. If the branch has to be bent downward from the trunk, ensure that the wire comes from below. If the branch is to be bent upwards, the wire should come from above.

Bending the Branches

Once the entire length of the tree has been wired, the branches can be bent and repositioned. In order to bend a branch. hold the outside of the branch with a finger and bend the rest of the branch from the curve with your thumbs. It is imperative to apply force gradually to reduce the risk of splitting. Once the branch has been positioned in an appropriate position, refrain from moving it. Repeated bending is likely going to damage the branches.

Guy-Wiring the Branches

One popular method of bending branches downward is guy-wiring for branches that are old, brittle or thick enough to be bent using coiled wire. The guy wire needs to be anchored on sturdy points like a strong surface root, a robust branch, or even a pot. A guy wire is usually thin, about one millimeter.

BEST TIME TO WIRE A BONSAI

There are no fast and hard rules for the time frame to wire a bonsai. A generally accepted time frame is three to five years. In this regard, just ensure that the tree's roots have carefully grown and the trunk is growing as well.

The time of year in which you start wiring your bonsai will depend on the tree species. The deciduous tree can be wired early in the spring. Coniferous trees, on the contrary, require wiring during late autumn or early winter.

Another important note about wiring is to wait until repotting because it will expedite the stability of the growing process. It is also a good idea to report before wiring because the plant will not be disturbed while the wires are in place.

WHEN TO REMOVE THE WIRES FROM BONSAI?

There is no rule in regard to leaving the wire on the trees. It depends solely on the growth of the tree and the degree of bend you have made. If the tree is young and vigorous, then the wire will bite into the branch sooner.

Bigger bends also tend to set sooner than subtle bends. If the tree is thin-barked, the wire may have to be removed in as little as six weeks. Older and more slow-growing trees could take six to nine months. However, rough-barked trees should be left with the wire for longer periods.

STYLE OF BONSAI

There are numerous styling forms of wiring the bonsai. These include:

Formal Upright Style

Bonsai grown in this style are reminiscent of trees that grow in nature within an open location without stress. In this type of tree, the trunk line is kept in a vertical direction. The apex is located just over the center of the base of the trunk. The trunk must taper from base to apex in this style.

Informal Upright Style

The most popular style of bonsai is the informal upright style. In order to create this style, bonsai artists start with trees that already have signs of stress imposed on them. The tree depicts elements of suffering as the trunk line shows contortion and the branches sag.

Slanting Style

Some trees in nature are tilted to one side by forces of wind or water, and some lean at an angle reaching for sunlight. These trees are usually equipped with a robust root system to cater to the weight of the tree's slant on the opposite side.

Double Trunk Style

This style basically depicts a tree with two trunks. The trunks are usually of two trees with different diameters that begin growing at the base. The two trees are then styled as one.

Styles of Bonsai Trees

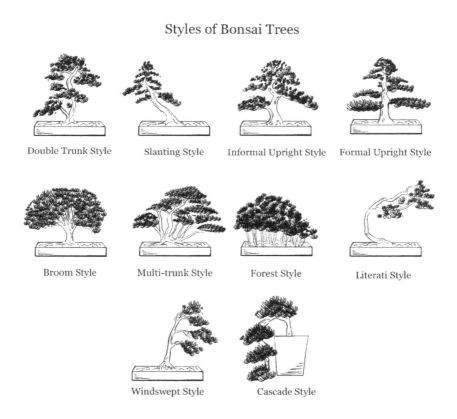

Double Trunk Style   Slanting Style   Informal Upright Style   Formal Upright Style

Broom Style   Multi-trunk Style   Forest Style   Literati Style

Windswept Style   Cascade Style

Literati Style

The literati style of a bonsai shows the essence of the tree. A literati is equipped with a robust and unique trunk line that is esthetically pleasing. Branches tend to be kept at a minimum. This style is often considered to be the most difficult to achieve.

Forest Style

The forest style of bonsai looks like a multi-trunk tree, but the difference is that it is composed of several trees rather than a singular one with multiple trunks. The most mature trees should be planted amid large and shallow pots. On the sides, smaller trees are planted, which contribute to a singular crown. The trees tend to be planted in a staggered pattern rather than a straight line. In this manner, the forest appears more realistic and natural.

Multi-Trunk Style

In theory, the multi-trunk style is similar to the double-trunk style, but it has three or more trunks. All trunks in this style grow out of a single root system, which truly becomes one tree. All the trunks contribute to one crown of leaves, which have thick and developed trunks forming the top.

Broom Style

This style is ideal for deciduous trees that have extensive and fine branching. The trunk is straight and upright. It does not reach the top of the tree and branches in all directions at almost one-third the tree's height.

Cascade Style

This form of tree is grown in tall pots since, for bonsai trees, it is difficult to maintain a downward-growing tree. The difficulty is primarily because the direction of growth is opposite the tree's natural tendency to grow upright. While growing a cascade-style tree, it is important to remember that it will grow upright for a small stretch and then bend downwards. The crown for this tree commonly grows above the edge of the pot, with subsequent branches alternating left and right on the main S-shaped trunk.

Windswept Style

The windswept style has branches and trunks going towards one side. This appears as though the wind has been blowing the tree in a singular direction. The branches grow on all sides of the trunk but eventually have to be bent towards one side.

Now that you have ample knowledge about wiring, it is time to analyze the health of the bonsai. In the next chapter, we will talk about maintaining bonsai's health.

9

MAINTAINING BONSAI HEALTH

S uppose you are enthusiastic about bonsai and artistically designing their esthetic. In that case, it is time you learn that you are not alone. One of the most famous bonsai collectors in the world is bonsai master Masahiko Kimura. His varied collection is one of a kind and eminent in nature. Kimura started at the age of fifteen, when he was apprenticed to Motosuke Hamano of Toju-en Bonsai Garden.

His passion gave his bonsai collection heights that the world has never seen. If you are starting in the pursuit of mastering the art of bonsai nurturing, then fret not. This chapter is specifically dedicated to ways through which the health of a bonsai can be maintained.

In this chapter, we will talk about weeds, fungi, and pests that impede the growth of a bonsai. Moreover, we will also walk through ways by which these problems can be catered to.

HOW TO REMOVE WEEDS

Weeds are often found growing within bonsai pots. Their removal is necessary not only because of their unsightliness but also because of the moisture and nutrients they steal from the soil of a bonsai plant.

Weeds find their way into a pot extremely easily since they are blown by the wind onto the surface of the soil. Weeds themselves, or their seeds, can also be present in the soil used at repotting time, particularly if organic soil components like leaf mold, bark, or sphagnum moss have been used.

WAYS TO REMOVE WEEDS FROM THE SOIL

Ideally, weeding needs to be carried out by hand; however, if a weed becomes established in the pot, its roots can quickly entangle with bonsai's. As a result, if you pull out the weed, it will also negatively impact the bonsai.

Moreover, removing weeds leads to a disturbance in the soil structure, since weeds can take away the soil with them, leaving voids and air pockets within the bonsai pot.

In this light, it is important to note that the complete removal of an established weed during the growing season is difficult. Especially, doing so without managing the bonsai is basically impossible.

The more unfortunate aspect of weed removal is that if the whole system of the weed is not removed, the weed species can regenerate and possibly reappear at a later date. A more simple and popular way of weed removal, therefore, is spraying a weedkiller.

Weedkillers

One of the most common ways of removing weeds includes using an herbicide, also known as a weedkiller. These serve the purpose of killing the weed by entering the green tissue of the leaves, then traveling within the weed until they reach the root system. Upon this entry, the weedkiller disrupts the root growth and activity.

HOW TO IDENTIFY PESTS AND BUGS

Another impedance that prevents bonsais from gaining their full potential is pests. However, these need to be identified beforehand so that accurate measures to cater to them can be taken. This chapter section will walk through some common pests and bugs.

Spider Mites

If you see tiny, oval-shaped mites about pinhead size scurrying around, these are spider mites. These can be identified by the yellow speckles on leaf surfaces. If you feel your bonsai is infested with them, then turn a leaf over.

If larger infestations are successfully made, the leaves of the bonsai will turn brown and die soon. Spider mites are essentially small and can be hard to spot, but an easy way to ascertain their presence is to hold a sheet of white paper under the branches. Then flick or gently shake the leaves. You'll be able to spot the mites as they drop down onto the paper.

White Flies

They are white flies if you see tiny, pure white "moths" resting on the leaf surface. These moth-like flies will flutter up and settle back down on the plant if disturbed. Infestation with white flies will make leaves look shiny with honeydew. Clear or white "scales" on the underside of the leaves can also be seen through a magnifier. All stages of whiteflies suck the plant juice.

Aphids

If your plant looks wilted and isn't thriving, it could be infested with aphids. To recognize aphids, you will have to look closely. If there are pear-shaped insects, especially on tender growing tips and undersides, then the infestation is by aphids.

Mealybugs

If the bonsai plant has distorted weak leaves, there is probably an infestation of mealybugs. A cluster of mealybugs looks like a cottony mass. These are often soft-bodied and slow-moving.

Thrips

If the leaf surface of your bonsai is finely speckled with yellow spots, there is a chance of thrips infestation. Once their growing stage is complete, the leaves will have a silvery-looking sheen covering them up. Not all thrips create this sheen, but black spots can be easily seen even without it.

Fungus Gnats

If small dingy gray flies fly around the bonsai aimlessly, these are fungus gnats. If the "flies" are seen arising out of the soil, these are fungus gnats. These are common with bonsai trees due to the constant watering and, as a result, moist soil conditions.

HOW TO KILL PESTS AND BUGS

There are a few ways through which bugs can be removed from bonsai trees. Some common methods include.

- Utilizing a solution of rubbing alcohol with water
- Use of neem oil
- Pesticides and insecticides
- Use of garlic
- Use of essential oils
- Usage of water bags
- Use of diatomaceous earth
- Using vinegar
- Water blasting

- Parasitic wasps and insects
- Manual removal of bugs

REMOVAL OF PESTS AND BUGS

The most natural way through which bad bugs can be killed is by the introduction of good bugs. Ladybugs are capable of feasting on spider mites. Another option is the usage of organic pesticides; however, a better option is to use a stream of water to blast the spider mites away from the plant. The latter is best suited for trees that are sturdy in nature.

A class of fungus, beauveria bassiana, is ideal for breaking through the insect's cuticle and killing it. Insecticidal soap with fatty acid works best for aphids, mealybugs, whiteflies, and thrips. Ladybugs are also ideal for aphids on plants.

How to Utilize Rubbing Alcohol and Water When Getting Rid of Bugs

In order to remove bugs from a bonsai plant, there are some common methods that you could adopt. One of the best things about alcohol and this technique is the majority of the ingredients are available in homes. This method is effective and works for almost every bug infestation you will ever encounter as a bonsai enthusiast.

Rubbing alcohol can be used in the following way:

- Move your bonsai away from the rest of your collection
- Take 1 cup of 70% rubbing alcohol
- Fill a bowl with 30 ounces of water

- Get a tablespoon of liquid soap
- Mix all these items in a bowl
- Once mixed, pour them all into a spray bottle
- Spray a small section of the tree and wait two days to make sure the solution does no damage
- If there's no damage, cover the soil and spray the bonsai thoroughly. Beware that getting alcohol onto the roots can have a drying effect.

The rubbing alcohol should be able to get rid of most bugs; however, if some are still left, then the procedure can be repeated up to two or three times.

How to Utilize Rubbing Alcohol and Cotton Wool

Like the previous method, this one also utilizes rubbing alcohol. However, this method requires a bit more force. This is important because some areas of the bonsai can be particularly hard to reach. In such a scenario, simply rubbing alcohol over the bonsai plant is not enough. For insects and bugs that are extremely small, this method works much better.

In order to utilise this method, do the following:

Pour 70% rubbing alcohol onto a cotton ball. Using this cotton ball, rub down every individual leaf, branch, and twig of your bonsai, along with the hard-to-reach areas like the underside of the leaves.

Target the bugs that are easy to spot directly. Once done, pour rubbing alcohol onto a cotton swab to reach all the nooks of the plant. This will be a lot easier than using a cotton ball.

Finish the process by rubbing alcohol into a paper towel and wiping it down the side of the pot, which can be a potential breeding ground for insects and eggs.

How to Get Rid of Bugs Using Neem Oil

An effective solution for removing pests like spider mites from bonsai trees is neem oil. In order to use it effectively, simply put the neem oil into a spray bottle and spray your plant, making sure to cover every part of the plant, including the underside of the leaves.

Once the pests have been removed, be sure to wash the bonsai to remove any excess neem oil. Once it is washed off completely, neem oil can also benefit any fungal root issue usually common in bonsai.

Neem oil has been found to be one of the most efficient ways to remove pests. The best element about neem oil is that it is a rare pesticide with 100% natural ingredients. The EPA has recognized it as a pesticide that does not lead to any adverse effects in humans. Not to forget, Neem is also OMRI listed, which is an accredited body within the USA that lists only organic produce. While neem oil is super effective against spider mites and fruit flies, it is not as effective against the good bugs called bees.

In order to improve the efficiency of this pesticide, there are certain elements can be added. Some tips that you could incorporate while using neem oil include:

Application of neem oil should be after sunset because it leads to overheating of the plant if given beforehand.

Among the various brands, choose one that is 100% organic at around 70% concentration level. Make sure that the neem oil contains Azadirachtin, which is an active ingredient in neem trees.

Using Pesticides and Insecticides

While pesticides and insecticides are not the most popular options to be used when removing bugs, they tend to be super effective. Like any other pesticides and insecticides, these work by poisoning the bugs that can wreak havoc on the bonsai. The insecticides release enzymes that affect bugs' nervous systems and lead to their ultimate demise.

The majority of insecticides and pesticides use organophosphates that are thoroughly regulated by the EPA to ensure that they are safe to be used by humans. When choosing a chemical pesticide, you will find a lot of ingredients in each.

However, the key ingredients that you should focus on are as follows, so make sure that the pesticide you choose has at least one of these:

- Diazinon
- Fenthion

- Malathion
- Methyl-parathion
- Sulfotep
- Trichlorfon

While using insecticides or pesticides, it is appropriate to take some precautions into consideration. Using pesticides can cause significant issues like skin rash if precautions are not taken. Some things you could consider include the following:

When using pesticides be sure to use thick gloves along with a mask. Once the spraying has been done, make sure that you are not in the same room if you are treating the plants indoors. Follow the instructions as listed on the bottle, as different pesticides often need to be used in different ways. Air out the rooms thoroughly before walking into the same room again that is used for spraying the bonsai. After using a pesticide or insecticide, be sure to take off clothes and wash them thoroughly. Wash your hands adequately after spraying.

While traditional insecticides and pesticides are effective, it is deemed that natural insecticides like neem oil tend to perform better without any side effects on an individual's skin.

Using Garlic to Get Rid of Bugs from a Bonsai Tree

Garlic is a common household item that can be used effectively to prevent bugs from getting hold of bonsai. Yes, the everyday garlic that is often found in the kitchen and in the ingredients of many dishes.

BONSAI FOR BEGINNERS | 141

Garlic, in particular, is very effective against aphids, and planting some garden garlic near the bonsai works best. Alternatively, if there isn't room or space, then consider planting individual cloves of garlic, which also act as natural repellents. You can choose to simply place them in the topsoil.

While this may not kill any bugs, it will surely stop them from making a permanent home out of your bonsai. Another good alternative is a garlic spray that can be made by simply mixing the garlic with water and spraying it onto the bugs directly. Once completed, be sure to wipe down the bonsai with fresh water.

Soapy Water for Aphids

Another popular DIY home remedy for aphids is soapy water. It is safe, natural, and extremely cheap to make. It is highly likely, in fact, that you have all the items to make it at home. It is also relatively safe for bonsai plants as long as the first spray test has been in a controlled spot.

Checking on a controlled spot means you will have to spray it onto a single leaf and then wait for some days before checking for burns or damage. If the plant seems visibly okay, apply the aphid killer to the entire tree.

How to Make the Insecticide for Aphids

Now that you understand the insecticide solutions that can be made at home for aphids, it is time to create your own mixture.

Ingredients:

- Tablespoon of dish detergent
- Three cups of water
- Spray bottle

How to make it:

Remember not to spray the mixture directly on the soil since the solution will be hard to remove. You can use a cotton ball or swab to apply the mixture rather than spray it directly. This will allow you to have more control over where the spray goes.

Getting Rid of Whiteflies

Another bug found on bonsai trees is whitefly. These flies, as previously discussed, are tiny but still visible. Whiteflies usually appear as tiny triangles. If disturbed, they fly around like regular flies. These are quick but clumsy and easy to kill.

If whiteflies have infested your tree, you will see a bunch of white eggs at the bottom of the leaves of your bonsai, or you may notice that a sticky substance is oozing from there. Both these signs are vital to consider the probability of a whitefly infestation.

Despite their name being "whitefly", these are more like aphids than any other pest. Whiteflies tend to fly around the bonsai and eat the leaves while extracting nutrients from the plant.

Adult whiteflies lay effects on the bottom of leaves that eventually become full adults in a matter of sixteen days.

A whitefly is capable of laying down hundreds of eggs that are only visible in a circular pattern. If enough resources are available at their disposal, the whitefly is capable of producing thousands more. Most whiteflies can be found around warm climatic areas. They eat fruits, vegetables, and ornamental plants like bonsai.

Whiteflies are destructive pests in nature. These tend to extract nutrients from leaves and behind them is a trail of sticky honeydew. This sticky substance eventually develops into a black fungus with a mold-like appearance.

The honeydew then covers the attacked plant to the extent that it can no longer photosynthesize. In other words, the plant can no longer create its own food, and as a result, its source of nourishment diminishes. The result is that the plant starts to wilt in a matter of days.

If you feel that there is a whitefly infestation on your bonsai, then the following are some key measures that you can take:

Remove the Affected Leaves.

The first thing you will have to do is prune all the leaves that demonstrate signs of whitefly infestation. Remove any leaves that show the whitefly has eaten them, whitefly eggs or leaves that appear to have wilted. This will help kill a large proportion of their population. Be sure to dispose of these leaves but first make sure to soak it in a cup containing rubbing alcohol. Dish soap can be used as an alternative to kill a whitefly.

Next, you need to remember that whiteflies are sensitive creatures that tend to create a flurry blur if you get close to them. So, instead of approaching them, you can let them come to you directly. You can place a small sticky trap around the plant to catch and kill them. These traps can be brought commercially, or can be made by you.

Another option is to make your own insecticide with soap. As previously discussed, you will need to add dish soap to a gallon of water. Spraying this mixture directly on the plant is lethal enough to kill them. Just make sure that you have targeted all the areas they can hide in. Be sure to look specifically under the leaves. Rinse the plant thoroughly after applying soap to eliminate the chemical toxins.

Be sure to not leave the dish soap mixture on the bonsai for too long, as it can harm the plant if you do not rinse it off properly. Be sure to first test the mixture by applying just a small amount of it on a limited area to check the damage.

To wash off the mixture, you will be using a hose with a powerful stream. This will blast them off completely as they reach their vulnerable state. This is best done once a layer of insecticidal soap has been applied thoroughly to the plant.

In this manner, you will be able to remove any dead whiteflies and clean up the excess soap present on the plant. The hose steam will remove any pests that have infested your plant and work extremely well for bugs on the bonsai.

Parasitic Wasps

One of the most commonly used predators for pest control are parasitic wasps. These are wasps that can be used to prey on whiteflies. These wasps do not sting, so they are safe to handle. These can be purchased online and then released in the greenhouse with your bonsai. Once released, the wasps will work on your plant's pest infestation. Other bugs that can be used include lacewings and beetles.

Other effective wasps include:

- Chalcid wasps
- Braconid wasps

Keep in mind these wasps can be bought online, or these can be attracted to the yard natively.

How to attract wasps

If you currently reside in an area where wasps are present, here are a few ways through which you can attract them:

Plant flowers: Using a variety of flowers so wasps can have plenty of pollen and nectar is a great way to attract them. Some common flowers and plants that you can use include alyssum, parsley, daisies, cilantro, and drill plants.

Provide water: Wasps need water and you can use small, shallow containers to supply plenty of it. Small tubs and pools can be utilised to attract them.

If the bonsai is already placed outdoors, place it near the parasitic wasps so they can eat the bugs on the plant. Remember that small river rocks should be placed above water level so that wasps can land on them. This method will be efficient in attracting them and allowing them to drink in your yard.

FUNGUS

Various kinds of fungi are harmful to bonsai plants. Some of the most common that you need to watch for are listed below:

Black Spot

This form of fungus usually attacks the foliage and will appear as a black spot or patch on leaves. Eventually, it will make the leaves yellow, shrivel and drop off. Once a leaf has been infected, it will need to be removed from the tree to prevent spreading. To cater to this situation, it is important to spray healthy foliage with a fungicide.

Leaf Spot

Similar to black spot diseases, this fungus is characterized by white, black, brown, or gray spots (the color varies according to the species). Spots can appear on leaves, twigs or branches. Generally, blemishes will be white initially and then change to dark color as the disease progresses. Remove any affected foliage immediately.

Mold or Mildew

Mildew is a type of fungus or mold that grows in a damp environment when there is insufficient light and poor ventilation. A white (powdery mildew) or black (sooty mold) substance tends to appear on the foliage, stems, or branches and can, as a result, distort the growth or cause discoloration and loss of vigor or dieback.

It is not possible to remove mildew from a tree, and as a result, the infected foliage and shoots must be removed. The tree needs to be sprayed with a fungicide afterward to prevent reinfection. Black sooty mold can also be caused by aphids or scale insects.

Rust

This fungal disease looks a bit like rust, hence its name. It can appear as yellow, orange, red, or brown raised bumps underneath the leaves. Eventually, the leaves curl up and fall. Although rust infections are not fatal, they can lead to severe damage. It is imperative to remove the affected area and treat the healthy foliage with a fungicide to prevent spread.

Chlorosis

This condition is caused by a lack of chlorophyll and results from a damaged or compacted root system along with nutrient deficiencies like a lack of iron. Leaves will turn yellow, but the veins will stay green, and the plant will begin to wilt.

Root Rot

Improper drainage can lead to roots turning brown and mushy. Leaves will become discolored, branches may weaken and break off, and the growth will also be stunted.

HOW TO TREAT A FUNGAL INFECTION

Lime Sulfur

Also known as Calcium polysulfide, this liquid is basically a chemical combination of lime (like the one in cement or garden lime) and elemental sulfur, and smells like rotten eggs. As a fungicide, lime sulfur can only be used on dormant trees due to the caustic nature of this chemical. While trees are dormant, in the form of deciduous trees, there is no tender tissue to damage, and in the case of most conifers, their adaptations to winter tend to protect them from the damage of lime sulfur.

Lime sulfur is also known to be one of the best ways to treat needle scales on pines and junipers since it kills the overwintering eggs of these insects. Lime sulfur should be applied at a specific rate depending on the application's reason. Suppose you decide to apply lime sulfur as a dormant spray during winter. In that case, 20:1 dilution with water to lime sulfur (equivalent to about three-quarters of a cup per gallon) is an appropriate dilution.

Keep in mind some species of conifers do not have tolerance towards the application of lime sulfur. Among these are many notable spruce species. Azaleas, for instance, also do not tolerate lime sulfur. Moreover, the application of lime sulphur without prior training and/or licensing is not allowed in some locations.

When a tree is first exposed to lime sulfur, the foliage turns yellow-orange, but when the sulfur evaporates, the foliage gets coated in a chalky white film. This white residue is the calcium that will normally wash off in a few weeks if you overhead water your plants regularly. On some deciduous tree species, it actually gives the appearance of older bark. Lime sulfur, however, has restrictions in some states, so it is important to check your local regulations.

Copper

Another commonly used fungicide is copper, which comes in different forms. It can be an effective treatment for the prevention of fungal infections in the bonsai foliage. Copper can be utilized as a dormant winter spray, but it can also be used in the growing season with little fear of damaging the foliage.

Copper, when it is present in fungicides, tends to interfere with many different aspects of fungal growth and reproduction. As a result, the development of copper resistance is highly unlikely. Copper also leaves minimally visible residue as a result of which it can be a good alternative to lime sulfur if one plans to show their trees in winter.

Copper sprays are mostly sold "ready to use" in the form of small spray bottles that require one to open the nozzle and

150 | HEAVENLY BONSAI

apply the spray to all the surfaces of the plant. Copper spray concentrates are available; one just needs to follow the instructions for dilution and spray all surfaces of leaves, twigs, and bark. Copper spray is normally not used for the purpose of root treatment.

Chlorothalonil

Sold as several different brands of garden fungal control and commonly called "Daconil", chlorothalonil is another fungicide that can be used. Chlorothalonil is a barrier to infection, and its application should be repeated regularly until conditions that favor fungal growth subside. It provides good measures of prevention of fungi but has a limitation in terms of treatment for existing problems.

Daconil tends to leave a white residue on leaves and needles. To provide effective control, try to avoid washing the residue off the leaves and reapply after significant rainfall.

FERTILIZER

Which fertilizer should be used? The best fertilizer for bonsai is a slow or continuous-release fertilizer. Generally, a balanced fertilizer that has nitrogen, phosphate, and potassium is the best option. This mixture will provide the plant with everything that is required to flourish.

PELLET OR LIQUID FERTILIZER

Pellet fertilizers are slow-release in nature and can last up to a year. Liquid fertilizers, on the other hand, are ideal as well; however, their quantity may vary for indoor and outdoor plants. Indoor plants may only need one-quarter to one-half teaspoon per gallon of water. In contrast, outdoor plants may require one-half teaspoon per gallon of water following watering.

WHEN SHOULD THE BONSAI BE FERTILIZED?

Regular fertilizing for a healthy bonsai is important, but the frequency may change with the season. Typically, trees should be fertilized from early spring to autumn, with some species requiring periodic feedings during non-growing months.

Tropical and subtropical trees require weekly fertilization during the growing season. Deciduous bonsai, too, require fertilization weekly in the growing season; however, it needs to be halted when the tree reaches dormancy. Conifers require fertilization weekly during the growing season. During winter, the fertilization schedule is limited to once or twice a month.

WHEN SHOULD FERTILIZATION BE AVOIDED?

A tree should not be fertilized when distressed. A distressed tree is one that is sick, newly repotted, or in need of watering. If repotting, one should wait at least a month for your tree to re-establish before reintroducing fertilizer.

OBTAINING FERTILIZER FOR BONSAI

The fertilizer can be obtained through the following;

- Hardware store
- bonsai Nurseries
- Online

Now that you know about various fertilizers and pests, it is time to turn the focus toward the death of bonsai. The next chapter explores how a bonsai can be prevented from dying and how it can be revived.

10

A BONSAI IN DISTRESS

A s a bonsai hobbyist, you will often encounter questions on bonsai care. These include caring for the health of the plant and nurturing it properly. Unfortunately, due to various reasons, a bonsai can die. In this chapter, we will discuss all the bases in detail, along with methods of revival.

BONSAI ROOTS

The roots of any tree are the basis of its life. While growing a bonsai is an art, catering to its roots is equally essential. Bonsai trees do not generally die overnight. One will start noticing warning signs of trouble early on, and correcting them beforehand is possible. Some warning signs of root death are as follow.[1]

Discoloration

There are many physiologic or normal reasons for a tree's colors to change, including seasonal change. But if the foliage of the tree begins to change color for no apparent reason, it could be a cause for concern.

Brittle Branches and Foliage

Another red flag that one should pay heed to is when the consistency of the foliage changes from soft and pliable to hard and brittle. The branches of a bonsai tree can get brittle as well. If you observe that the branches that once used to be soft and pliable are now brittle, it could signify bonsai dying.

WAYS TO CHECK

If the tree is discoloured or brittle, then check to see if the tree is alive. There are simple ways to do it without any special tools.

The Fingernail Test

A tree's bark protects the life underneath it. In order to see if a particular branch is still alive, all that is needed is to remove a small portion of the top brown bark to see if the next layer is green.

Remember, green is the color of life. In order to perform the fingernail test, you would need to scrape off a small portion of the bark with your fingernail. If there is no green under the surface, keep scratching. If you reach the hardwood and there is no green, the tree is dead.

Dead Branches

If a branch on the tree is dead, it is not a bad thing in all essence. Often dead branches are also called "deadwood," and they become a tree feature. In fact, the juniper bonsai have considerable deadwood incorporated in their design.

The deadwood is often dyed white to contrast with the living tissue that remains. Bark usually falls off after some time, exposing smooth wood underneath. It is a warning sign if you find large areas of smooth wood on an old branch.

HOW TO REVIVE A DYING BONSAI TREE

A dying bonsai can be a detrimental event in the life of bonsai hobbyists. One may want to revive the bonsai if one can. The following are some possibilities for revival.

Step 1: Prune Dead Sections

Use sharp, sterile pruning shears to remove areas of the bonsai that cannot be Saved, like dead or broken branches, wilted foliage, and stems. Cut the branches back to the trunk or leader.

Step 2: Check the Inside

Look to see if the cut stems are green on the inside. If the insides of the stem are green and healthy, then you can expect the bonsai to revive and regrow. If some areas of the interior are dry while others are not, there is no need to panic.

Step 3: Prune the Roots

Remove the bonsai from its container to root-prune and repot it. Inspect the root system thoroughly. Using sterile and sharp shears, prune away the dead and wilted roots.

Step 4: Place in Water

Place the bonsai within a clean clear container filled with luke-warm water covering the root system. Then clean the container and create a soil mixture while the bonsai rests in the water.

Step 5: Prepare Container and Soil

Wash the container with mild detergent and warm water. Ensure that any particles stuck on the inside of the container are removed. Choose an open and porous soil mixture with good retentive qualities.

Step 6: Repot the Bonsai

Cover the drainage holes with a mesh or coffee filter and fill the container a third of the way. Position the bonsai and fill the remaining container with soil. Allow your bonsai to sit in water by placing it in a sink or bucket of water.

Step 7: Choose a Prime Location

Remove the bonsai from water and allow water to drain through drainage holes. Place the bonsai in a location with four to six hours of sunlight or a different amount suited for the species. Choose a location that is well ventilated. If the overnight temperature of the location stays above 40 degrees Fahrenheit, the bonsai can stay outdoors. In winter, it should be placed in a south-facing window if possible.

Step 8: Water the Bonsai

Irrigate the bonsai with water regularly as the soil dries over the top. Allow the soil to dry slightly in between irrigations to avoid over-watering. If the soil is dry about a half inch deep, water the bonsai to prevent the roots from drying out.

Step 9: Give the Bonsai Time

The bonsai takes some time to regenerate its lost cells. It may take until the following growing season for signs of revitalization to show.

MISTAKES THAT LEAD TO THE DEATH OF BONSAI

There are certain mistakes that lead to the death of a bonsai plant. Some of the errors that can be avoided include:

#1 – Forgetting to Water

Bonsai trees are ideally planted in small pots, which naturally do not leave enough nutrients and water reserves. If a person forgets to water their bonsai, it will dry up and eventually die.

The roots can be figured out as having dried out when the soil is absolutely dry, and the leaves will begin withering and falling off. If you have an evergreen plant, its foliage will slowly turn yellow. If the roots have dried up completely, the tree cannot be saved. However, if the roots are not completely dry, the tree can be rescued by watering it correctly and following an appropriate care routine.

#2 – Placing an Outdoor Tree Species Indoors

The first thing you'll have to do in this regard is identify the tree species and the location where it needs to be placed. Indoor bonsai should be ideally placed at a south-facing window, and outdoor bonsai should get plenty of light and protection from strong winds.

#3 – Over-Watering

The soil mixture for bonsai plays an essential role in its survival. If a person chooses a soil mixture that retains a lot of water, they will be bound to frequent watering. The downside to regular watering is that it will keep the soil wet but rot the roots and eventually kill the plant. The watering of bonsai is a two-edged sword because over-watering can kill it slowly, but neglecting water will kill it in days.

#4 – Insufficient Light

A majority of bonsai, if not all, are subtropical trees. This implies that they require a lot of light to survive. Most homes do not receive adequate sunlight, so placing the plant in a south-facing window is essential.

Outdoor bonsai have the same light requirements as other trees. A lack of light will cause the tree to "stretch" toward a light source. It is appropriate to use shade cloth or place the pots in a light shade.

#5 – Lack of Patience

Beginners are usually over-enthusiastic about redesigning their trees every other week. They tend to over-prune their trees and wire extremely often. As a result, the trees cannot keep up with the rate of change. To avoid this mistake, one should remember that big changes to a bonsai, like repotting or significant pruning, should be done only once a year.

Now that you know why a bonsai is in distress and ways to revive it, the next part is how a bonsai can be grown with an esthetic sense in mind.

11

ESTHETICS AND MAINTENANCE

Bonsai's esthetics are why people around the globe are over-zealous about them. One such exhibition in Japan is the Taikan-ten exhibition. The Itoigawa Juniper at this exhibition is extremely beautiful and is one of the major attractions of Kyoto, Japan.

In this chapter, we will explore the esthetic of a bonsai and how a bonsai can be placed in a manner that is pleasing to the eye in the sense of appearance.

BONSAI ESTHETIC

The esthetic of a bonsai is one of the core elements when one starts nurturing the plant. Following are some factors of the esthetic that should be considered.

SIGNIFICANCE OF CULTURE

Depending upon the cultural beliefs of a person, the bonsai tree can serve as a symbol of harmony, balance, patience, or even luck. Most individuals around the globe use potted trees as living ornaments for interior design.

EMPHASIS

One common aim in the designing of a bonsai is depicting an ideal. In the esthetic of a bonsai, there is a "focal design point", which is an exaggeration or emphasis of one of the features. It is interesting to develop and exciting to view an archetypal.

PERSONIFICATION

Artistry in bonsai and other aspects of the world is an effort to imbue our work with human qualities. In every human work, whether a painting or a bonsai tree, one tries to personify human qualities in work. The degree of success one has in conveying these qualities through artistic work is directly proportional to the artistic success of the work.

SPECIES-SPECIFIC DESIGN

In terms of bonsai design, it is common that certain species of tree are styled like other bonsai of that species. For example, it is common to see Cryptomeria japonica styled in a formal upright form and seldom in any other style. Zelkova serrata is styled in a broom form, usually. These are examples of species-specific styling.

BONSAI DISPLAY—TOKONOMA

The practice of displaying a bonsai does not have to be complex. As a bonsai enthusiast, one may be intrigued about presenting it in the best way possible. There are a lot of issues to consider, but three critical points should always serve as your guide.

1. The paramount element of the display must be the bonsai. The selection of bonsai should drive every decision one makes about the display.
2. The bonsai display should look natural and call forth feelings of harmony.
3. Every part of the display should serve a purpose. Nothing within it is unimportant.

SELECTION OF BASIC ITEMS

Since bonsai, in its essence, is rooted in a celebration of nature, every element selected should also be based upon nature. This would imply selecting a bonsai plant that displays some particular aspects of its beauty for the current season.

The Pot

Once the bonsai has been selected, one can start contemplating the pot. The color of the pot needs to be harmonious with the state of the bonsai. The ideal width of a pot is the width of the spread of bonsai's branches. The ideal depth of a pot is dependent on whether the bonsai cascades. If a bonsai is non-cascading, the pot's depth should be approximately the size of the bonsai's roots just above its flare.

The Stand

Bonsai can be best viewed at eye level, which means that the average table will be too low. A bonsai stand or "shoku" can either be a floor stand or a table stand. The stand itself should not be ornamental so as not to distract the attention from the bonsai. Like the pot, the color of the stand should be in harmony with the state of the bonsai.

The Placement of the Display

The placement of the display is different from the placement of elements within the display. This includes selecting where the entire display should be presented. Remember, nothing in the display should be an afterthought.

Selecting Companion Objects

Before finalizing the companion object, create a natural scene in your mind about what you want it to look like. The companion objects should be selected based on their ability to contribute and enhance the scene. Again, the major guide should be nature. If the plan is to display the bonsai with a small flowering plant or statue, it should be one that is seen naturally occurring with the bonsai.

Finally, do not select too many companion objects; two objects should be the maximum limit.

Placing Elements within the Display

Now that everything has been finalized, picture the scenery you are trying to create. Remember that the elements need to be in a harmonious dimension and perspective.

The Bonsai

The typical shape of a display is an asymmetrical triangle. The bonsai should be placed on the side opposite to its pull. If the branches of a bonsai lean predominantly towards the right, one will place the bonsai on the left side.

The Companion Objects

A companion object should be placed on the opposite side of the area, away from the bonsai. Typically, a companion object should be present farthest from the nearest side wall of the bonsai. However, it should not be on the same horizontal axis either.

The companion object should be either behind or in front of the axis. If the companion object is stones, these will be placed towards the back wall, or if they are small flowering plants or statues, then they need to be placed farther away from the back wall than the bonsai.

Importance of Display Table

Bonsai display tables are as important as pots, stones, tools or humidity. They serve to protect whatever floor or carpeting is under them. They also add to the whole look of the bonsai area. A sense of formality can be achieved by the table, which sets the bonsai garden apart from the remainder of the room. This emphasises the time and care that have gone into the bonsai's creation.

Some of the best display tables are hand-carved by Chinese artisans who understand the artistic aspects of bonsai and the art of cultivating foliage within a garden. Ideally, these are made of hardwood that cradles the hard-won treasure elegantly.

CONCLUSION

Now that you have read it all, it is time to re-look at things from a different perspective. At the beginning of the book, we discussed the origins of the word bonsai. The Japanese term "Bon-Sai" means "planted in a container" when translated literally. This art style was inspired by a traditional Chinese horticultural technique, later modified by Japanese Zen Buddhism. This is why the original term for this ancient art was the Chinese word "pun-sai" or "penjing". *The pen* is the Chinese word for pot, while *Jing* means scenery or landscape. The art of bonsai has existed for over a millennium. Growing a bonsai is ultimately intended to provide a miniature yet accurate reflection of nature in the shape of a tree. And the best part is that bonsai trees can be grown from any tree!

The drainage of soil is another important aspect, with the requirements of each bonsai and its soil types varying. As we moved forward, we walked through the different kinds of pots available and whether or not to use a drip tray. Then we looked at some important tools for bonsai care.

Starting a bonsai is another important aspect; with knowledge available at the fingertips of bonsai enthusiasts, it is an easy journey forward. Not to forget the different watering requirements. Each species for each weather has different watering requirements.

After effectively growing a bonsai, it is time to structure it with wires. The time of wire removal is an important aspect that needs to be looked through thoroughly. Remember, plants need time, and take time to adjust to changes.

In caring for bonsai, you need to remember how to prune it effectively with consideration of the best season and branch selection in mind. Next, do not forget to cater for pests, fungi, and weeds.

Remember that bonsai, like any other plant, require immense care, and some mistakes can lead to early death. Be sure to observe the signs and symptoms of bonsai dying and try to revive the plant as soon as you can. Lastly, we walked through the esthetics and how the table and other elements of the display can be set effectively.

READER REVIEWS MATTER!

Your opinion is invaluable to us. If you've enjoyed reading our book and you're in the United States, we'd love to hear your thoughts on Amazon's review page. Simply scan the QR code below or visit (Amazon Review Page URL) to share your review.

Your feedback is a guiding light for fellow readers. Thank you for being a cherished member of our community!

https://amzn.to/47C5sjL

GLOSSARY

Acidic – Having qualities of acid, pH less than 7.

Accent Plant – A small plant which is displayed next to a bonsai. Accent plants typically tend to be used when a bonsai is formally displayed at a show or exhibition. Accent plants may include perennials, bamboo or grass.

Aeration – Allowing air to move through something. In the case of bonsai, it would be soil.

Esthetic – of, relating to, or dealing with esthetics or the beautiful.

Air Layering – A technique employed to force a tree or branch to form novel (new) roots at a certain point.

Akadama – This literally means clay soil and is an element that is heated to a high temperature, at which it changes its crystalline structure.

Alkaline – Having qualities of bases, pH more than 7.

Apex – The highest point or vertex of plant stem or root.

Argillaceous Rock – A class of sedimentary rock that contains clay components. If left untreated, it breaks down fairly readily due to the absorption of water, and its subsequent swelling then retracts and cracks into smaller components.

Bleeding – Loss of sap by a wound or because of puncturing.

Broad-Leaved/Coniferous – Conifers belong to a group of naked-seeded plants called gymnosperms. Their seeds are never enclosed in an ovary. The leaves of conifers tend to be needle-shaped or scale-like. All conifers are "evergreen", with a few notable exceptions. Broad-leaved trees are an extensive group that belongs to angiosperms or flowering plants that have seeds enclosed within an ovary. Also known as "deciduous" trees, these go dormant from autumn until spring.

Calcite – A colorless mineral which is composed of calcium carbonate.

Callus – Woody "scar" tissue that forms when a branch is pruned. The wound heals in the form of a callus. It's the healing process of the tree.

Chlorosis – Loss of chlorophyll that results due to mineral deficiency.

Chlorothaloni – An organic compound that is mainly used as a broad-spectrum fungicide.

Copper – Chemical element with symbol Cu

Conifer – A tree bearing cones, mainly evergreen trees such as pines, cedars, spruces and junipers. Coniferous trees have small and waxy leaves. Sometimes have just needles too, which they usually keep all year round.

Cut paste wound – A wound sealant typically made to promote healing and keep the sap from bleeding.

Deadwood – A special technique that is utilised to create deadwood on a bonsai that enhances the character and appearance of a tree.

Deciduous – These are broad-leaved trees that tend to harden off and shed their leaves during autumn with dormancy in winter.

Diatomaceous Earth – A sedentary soil that is produced by shells/skeletons of diatoms (not a volcanic activity, which is pumice). It is currently being used to replace akadama.

Evergreen – A plant type whose foliage remains green through more than one growing season.

Fired clay – A range of refractory clays used to make ceramics, especially fire bricks for pots.

Fungicide – A chemical compound that is utilised to prevent the growth and spread of fungus that can cause serious damage to bonsai.

Graft – A technique used to meld or attach a branch to the stump of a tree.

Internode – The section of growth between two nodes (leaves or leaf joints).

Jin – A Japanese term meaning part of a branch that is bare-stripped.

Lime sulfur – A mixture of calcium polysulfide and thiolsulfate, utilised in pest control.

Leader – The dominant upright stem, usually the cut-off trunk.

Nebari – A Japanese term describing roots of a tree that are visibly seen on the surface.

Neem oil – A vegetable oil extracted from fruits and seeds of neem.

Node – A growth point present on a branch or trunk from which leaves, leaf buds and shoots appear.

Peat – Organic soil component that is derived from rotted and broken-down sphagnum moss, unpopular with bonsai enthusiasts.

pH – Measure of soil acidity. pH measures the acidity or alkalinity of material dissolved in water, which is ranked on a scale of 0-14. The pH can be divided into ranges such as:

- pH 0 - 2 Most acidic
- pH 3 - 5 Acidic
- pH 6 - 8 Neutral zone
- pH 9 - 11 Alkaline
- pH 12 - 14 Most alkaline

Pot – A growing container for bonsai, usually it is high-fired clay.
Pruning – One of the most important methods of training a bonsai.
Ramification – The repeated division of branches into secondary branches by means of pruning.
Repotting – The practice of taking a pot-grown bonsai out of its prior container and placing it in a bigger one to encourage renewed growth. It is also a great time to refresh the soil.
Root pruning – The practice of cutting back on the roots when repotting the bonsai from one pot to another to encourage more growth.
Root rot – A disease infecting the roots growing in damp or wet soil.
Root over rock – A technique adopted when the tree is planted over a rock with roots extended downwards to reach the soil.
Seasonal Bonsai – A species that looks its ultimate best for only a short period of time when in flower or fruit.
Senescent – Old, growing old
Shari – Part of a live tree trunk that is barkless or has deadwood present.
Sphagnum moss – A general name given to a long fibered moss that is used as an organic soil component and air-layering. It has a great ability to absorb and hold moisture.
Under-watering – When a tree is dried up completely and is not watered when required.
Vermiculite – This is a mineral called mica which is heated and puffed up to form a lightweight, sponge-like granule that is capable of holding both water and air. It is useful in rooting seedlings.
Volcanic lava – It is an esthetic stone with great texture and hollows.
Wiring – This is a technique used to wire around a branch or trunk in a

certain direction during training to encourage its growth in a certain direction.

Wound sealant – A compound that is formatted to seal cuts that are remade on branches or on the trunk of a bonsai to prevent the loss of moisture and promote healing.

Japanese Bonsai Tree Styles

Banyan – A tree style that requires dramatically exposed roots that grow from branches and trunks while they reach down to the soil.

Literati – A bonsai tree form that has a tall, slender trunk with no lower branches and sparse foliage that is confined to the top of the tree.

General Japanese Bonsai Terms

Sekou – Root over rock

Shari – A technique utilised to create deadwood on the trunk

Shohin – Tiny things in Japan. It is a name commonly given to bonsai trees that are less than 6 inches (15 cm) in height.

NOTES

1. KON'NICHIWA BONSAI

1. https://www.oldest.org/nature/bonsai-trees/
2. https://www.oldest.org/nature/bonsai-trees/

2. THE SOIL AND NUTRITION

1. (Steven, n.d.)
2. (Steven, n.d.)
3. https://www.bonsaiempire.com/basics/bonsai-care/bonsai-soil
4. https://en.wikipedia.org/wiki/Capillary_action
5. https://www.kaizenbonsai.com/bonsai-tree-care-information/choosing-soil-for-bonsai-trees
6. https://www.kaizenbonsai.com/bonsai-tree-care-information/choosing-soil-for-bonsai-trees
7. (Bonsai, n.d.)
8. https://www.bonsaiempire.com/basics/bonsai-care/bonsai-soil
9. (Bonsai, n.d.)
10. https://www.bonsaiempire.com/basics/bonsai-care/bonsai-soil
11. (Bonsai, n.d.)
12. https://www.kaizenbonsai.com/bonsai-tree-care-information/choosing-soil-for-bonsai-trees#CHARACTERISTICS-OF-SOME-POPULAR-SOIL-COMPONENTS
13. https://www.bonsaiempire.com/basics/bonsai-care/bonsai-soil
14. https://www.bonsaiempire.com/basics/bonsai-care/bonsai-soil
15. (StackPath, n.d.)
16. https://www.kaizenbonsai.com/bonsai-tree-care-information/choosing-soil-for-bonsai-trees#CHARACTERISTICS-OF-SOME-POPULAR-SOIL-COMPONENTS
17. (Bonsaiplace, 2016)
18. (Bonsaiplace, 2016)

3. THINKING POTS

1. https://premierbonsai.co.uk/contents/en-uk/d2111895.html
2. (Parate, n.d.)
3. (BonsaiYard, 2022)
4. (BonsaiYard)
5. https://thegardeningcook.com/drainage-hole-covers/
6. (*Bonsai Pot Drip Trays | Bonsaischule Wenddorf*, n.d.)

4. TOOLS YOU NEED

1. (*Bonsai Tools and Materials - Bonsai Empire*, n.d.)
2. (*Bonsai Tools and Materials - Bonsai Empire*, n.d.)

5. HOW TO START A BONSAI

1. (*Buying Nursery Stock (Prebonsai) - Bonsai Empire*, n.d.)
2. (*How to Repot a Bonsai Tree - Advice - Westland Garden Health*, n.d.)
3. (*How to Repot a Bonsai Tree - Advice - Westland Garden Health*, n.d.)
4. (*Where to Place Your Bonsai Tree - Bonsai Empire*, n.d.)

7. PRUNING PRIORITIES

1. https://www.easternleaf.com/Bonsai-Cut-Paste-p/113710-01.htm

10. A BONSAI IN DISTRESS

1. (*How to Recognize Dead Wood and Branches*, n.d.)

REFERENCES

Bonsai pot drip trays. (n.d.). BONSAISCHULE WENDDORF. Retrieved October 10, 2022, from https://www.bonsai-shop.com/en/bonsaipots/drip-trays

Bonsai tools and materials. (n.d.). Bonsai Empire. https://www.bonsaiempire.com/basics/general/tools

Bonsai, E. (n.d.). *Choosing The Right Pot For Your Bonsai Tree.* Premierbonsai.co.uk. Retrieved October 10, 2022, from https://premierbonsai.co.uk/contents/en-uk/d2111895.html

Do Bonsai Pots Need Drainage Holes? (n.d.). – Bonsai Yard. www.bonsaiyard.com/general/do-bonsai-pots-need-drainage-holes/

Bonsai, K. (n.d.). *Choosing Soil for Bonsai Trees.* Www.kaizenbonsai.com. Retrieved October 10, 2022, from https://www.kaizenbonsai.com/bonsai-tree-care-information/choosing-soil-for-bonsai-trees

Bonsaiplace. (2016, May 22). *Soil pH and Bonsai.* Bonsaiplace. https://bonsaiplace.net/2016/05/22/soil-ph-and-bonsai/

BonsaiYard. (2022). *Do bonsai pots need drainage holes? (Bonsai specialist idea)* – *Bonsai Yard.* Bonsai Yard. https://www.bonsaiyard.com/general/do-bonsai-pots-need-drainage-holes/

Buying nursery stock (Prebonsai). (n.d.). Www.bonsaiempire.com. Retrieved October 10, 2022, from https://www.bonsaiempire.com/basics/cultivation/nursery-stock

Cook, R. (2018, November 29). *How to Create Bonsai from Regular Trees.* This Old House. https://www.thisoldhouse.com/gardening/21124721/how-to-create-bonsai-from-regular-trees

Ferwerda, J. (2020, May 3). *Bonsai material: Digging from a garden.* Growing Bonsai. https://www.growingbonsai.net/bonsai-material-digging-from-a-garden/

How to Recognize Dead Wood and Branches. (n.d.). The Spruce. Retrieved October 10, 2022, from https://www.thespruce.com/how-to-recognize-dead-wood-3269556

How to Repot a Bonsai Tree. (n.d.). Westland Garden Health. Retrieved October

10, 2022, from https://www.gardenhealth.com/advice/indoor-growing/ how-to-repot-a-bonsai-tree

(n.d.). Brainy Quote. https://www.brainyquote.com/quotes/ sloane_crosley_506259

Parate, P. (n.d.). *Bonsai Pots: The Ultimate Guide for Beginners*. Retrieved October 10, 2022, from https://abanahomes.com/bonsai-pot-guide/

Grand, A. (n.d.). *Bonsai Soil Requirements: How To Mix Soil For Bonsai Trees* . Www.gardeningknowhow.com. https://www.gardeningknowhow.com/ houseplants/bonsai/bonsai-soil-requirements.htm

Steven, R. (n.d.). *Requirements of Bonsai Soils - Bonsai Empire*. Www.bonsaiempire.com. Retrieved October 10, 2022, from https://www. bonsaiempire.com/blog/bonsai-soil-requirements

Where to place your Bonsai tree. (n.d.). Www.bonsaiempire.com. https://www. bonsaiempire.com/basics/bonsai-care/position

Made in the USA
Las Vegas, NV
06 December 2024

13510135R00098